Constitutional Law

Fourth Edition

Cavendish
Publishing
Limited

London • Sydney • Portland, Oregon

Fourth edition first published in Great Britain 2004 by
Cavendish Publishing Limited, The Glass House,
Wharton Street, London WC1X 9PX, United Kingdom
Telephone: + 44 (0)20 7278 8000   Facsimile: + 44 (0)20 7278 8080
Email: info@cavendishpublishing.com
Website: www.cavendishpublishing.com

Published in the United States by Cavendish Publishing
c/o International Specialized Book Services,
5824 NE Hassalo Street, Portland,
Oregon 97213-3644, USA

Published in Australia by Cavendish Publishing (Australia) Pty Ltd
45 Beach Street, Coogee, NSW 2034, Australia

Cataloguing in Publication Data
Data available

ISBN 1-85941-941-0

1 3 5 7 9 10 8 6 4 2

Typeset by Phoenix Photosetting, Chatham, Kent
Printed and bound in Great Britain

Contents

1 Introduction

Constitutional law is concerned with the role and powers of state institutions and with the relationship between the citizen and the state. In essence a state's constitution is the collection of rules that determines those roles and powers, and which provides safeguards to that relationship.

Purposes of a constitution

- Defines (limits) Government power.
- Guardian of fundamental rights.
- Provides a covenant, a symbol and aspiration for a nation.
- To deceive?

Definitions of a constitution

- **Narrow** – a single document or series of documents containing all the basic rules of a state.
- **Broad** – rules, wherever written or unwritten, that determine the creation and operation of governmental institutions.

If we define a constitution narrowly, as a written document or series of documents, then Great Britain has no constitution. However, if we take a broader definition of a constitution, namely, the existence of rules determining the creation and operation of governmental institutions, then clearly Great Britain has a constitution. It is not alone amongst modern democracies in its omission: Israel and New Zealand also have no central constitutional document.

The history: written or unwritten

When we think of a constitution we probably first think of a written document or series of documents. The seminal written constitutions were those that followed the American War of Independence (1775–83) and the French Revolution (1789). Following on from these examples, most modern democracies have adopted written constitutions in one form or another. A common characteristic of written constitutions is that they were drawn up to make a clear historical break with the past, frequently a break with previous imperial power.

Great Britain on the other hand, besides the constitutional upheavals of the second half of the 17th century, has seen no break in its constitutional history since 1066. Consequently, Britain's constitution is the product of a gradual and peaceful evolution. This evolution started with such historical legal documents as the Magna Carta (1215) and continues through to Acts of Parliament of the modern day, such as those establishing devolution and the Human Rights Act (1998). Since the Bill of Rights (1689), statute law has increasingly shaped the constitution. However, as we shall see, much of the constitution is rooted in the common law. For example, many of the central principles that govern the powers of state institutions and their relationship with the individual citizen have emerged from case law. Lastly, much of what is considered constitutional law is in fact non-legal conventions and practices, which have also developed from particular historical origins.

Characteristics of the UK constitution

This division between written and unwritten constitutions is somewhat superficial – no constitution is exclusively written or unwritten. There are more crucial differences we can identify between Britain's unwritten (or uncodified) constitution and the codified constitutions of most modern democracies.

Codified	Uncodified (Britain)
⮕ Determinate and distinct law	⮕ Indeterminate and indistinct law
⮕ Rigid/entrenched	⮕ Flexible/unentrenched
⮕ Overarching and planned	⮕ Growth through pragmatic incrementalism

Indeterminate and indistinct

Britain's constitution is a mixture of:

- statute;
- case law;
- political practices or conventions;
- detailed procedures.

But we cannot point precisely to what is or is not of constitutional relevance. In contrast to codified constitutions, there is nothing to distinguish constitutional law in the UK from any other law. For example, certain Acts of Parliament may be regarded as constitutionally important, such as the Acts of Union or the Human Rights Act, but these Acts are no different in status from the Dangerous Dogs Act.

'The Constitution is what the judges say it is', is a famous quote from a former Chief Justice of the US Supreme Court, Charles Evans Hughes. This is equally, if not more, apparent in the UK, where much of the constitution, and in particular the limits of governmental power, has or have been defined by the courts in case law. Nevertheless, English judges are unlikely to be so forthright.

Lastly, the UK's uncodified constitution is made even less determinate by the fact that much of it is governed by unwritten convention and practice that has evolved and continues to evolve over time. We shall look at conventions in more detail under 'Sources of the constitution', below.

Flexible/unentrenched

Whether a constitution is flexible or rigid is determined by the ease with which it can be amended. The constitutional laws under a codified constitution are invariably given special protection from subsequent appeal or amendment. That is to say, they are 'entrenched'. This may be by *full entrenchment*, such that the substance of certain laws can never be changed. For example, parts of German (Basic) Law are entrenched in this manner, such that they can never be repealed or amended unless there is a complete break with the existing legal order in Germany. Alternatively, there may be *partial entrenchment* by the inclusion of stringent procedures to be followed before any change may be made. For example, any amendment to the US Constitution must be proposed by a two-thirds majority in both houses of Congress, or by a national convention called at the request of two-thirds of the state legislatures. Once the change is proposed, it must be ratified by three-quarters of the state legislatures (Article V).

By comparison with this, the UK's constitution is highly flexible. As we shall see when looking at 'Parliamentary sovereignty' in Chapter 2 below, in theory there are no legal restraints on Parliament's powers – it can pass, repeal or amend any law by a simple majority. Importantly, no Parliament can lay down irreversible rules that bind future

Parliaments. We will examine non-legal and political restraints on Parliament, as well as restraints imposed by membership of the EU, later; however, at this stage, suffice it to say that no law can be 'legally' entrenched in the UK.

Growth through pragmatic incrementalism

The absence of a written constitution enables the body of constitutional law in the UK to be changed and added to with the minimum of constitutional formality. Consequently, the constitution has grown freely in response to the needs of the time. This has led to a gradual and pragmatic growth. On occasion changes may be very great, such as when the UK joined the European Communities in 1973. Changes more often will be less dramatic, for example, when a particular judgment is given in a case of constitutional importance.

Characteristics revealed in recent changes

The recent major constitutional changes undertaken by the Labour Government readily exemplify the flexible characteristics of the constitution. From the point of view of the constitutional law student, the general election of May 1997 is of considerable significance, in as much as it produced a Government committed to major constitutional reform. The reform programme in the 1997 Labour Manifesto included:

- incorporation of the European Convention on Human Rights into UK law;
- a Scottish Parliament;
- a Welsh Assembly;
- devolution for Northern Ireland;
- a strategic authority for London;
- reform of the House of Lords;
- modernisation of the House of Commons;
- new electoral systems;

- a Freedom of Information Act;
- more accountable and democratic local government;
- regional chambers leading to directly elected regional assemblies in England.

The Labour Government elected in May 1997 moved with extraordinary speed to implement this extensive programme. Amongst the raft of constitutional legislation, the following may be highlighted:

- the Human Rights Act 1998;
- the Scotland Act 1998;
- the Government of Wales Act 1998; and
- the Northern Ireland Act 1998.

Also, following a referendum in May 1998, the Greater London Authority Act was passed in November 1999, and the first elections for the Greater London Authority and London Mayor were held in May 2000. The first stage of the reform of the House of Lords was implemented by the House of Lords Act 1999. Electoral reform included the European Parliamentary Elections Act 1999, and local government reforms were made under the Local Government Act 2000. There was also the Freedom of Information Act, passed in November 2000.

However, not surprisingly, the whole of the 1997 Labour Manifesto's constitutional programme was not implemented in a single term. At the time of Labour's re-election on 7 June 2001, the following commitments to reform remained unfulfilled:

- second stage reform of the House of Lords;
- modernisation of the House of Commons;
- a referendum on voting system for the House of Commons;
- regional government in England.

In Labour's second term, there has been a certain 'cooling off' after the dramatic changes of the first term. The second stage of reform of the House of Lords has stalled, as outlined in Chapter 5. There have been limited measures introduced to modernise practices in the House of Commons, but the underlying issues of accountability and dominance of the executive have not been addressed, and are not likely to be. The crucial referendum on changing the voting system in the Commons has also been delayed indefinitely. As regards regional government in England, the Government introduced a White Paper, *Your Region, Your Choice*, and subsequently, in November 2002, the Regional Assemblies (Preparations) Bill into Parliament. However the reforms are still in their infancy. The Bill will enable regional referendums to be held, but the precise nature of the powers or functions regional assemblies would have, if they were established, is still undecided. Nonetheless, the constitution of the UK continues to grow through lesser but still important developments, such as the setting up of a new Department of Constitutional Affairs and the consequent removal of the Lord Chancellor's role in government. The significance of the reforms that have been undertaken and those yet to be completed will be considered in due course.

Sources of the constitution

In an unwritten constitution, as we have already said, it is difficult to be precise about which rules – statutory, common law or conventional – are to be included under 'constitutional' law. One cannot be expected to learn by rote a catalogue of all statutory, common law and conventional sources that bear upon constitutional issues. However, it is important to have a broad overview of the main elements that make up the constitution. The sources are commonly divided between the legal and non-legal.

Legal sources	Non-legal sources
⮑ Legislation ⮑ Case law ⮑ EU law ⮑ The Royal Prerogative	⮑ Conventions ⮑ Authoritative textbooks

Legal sources

Legislation

Legislation is of primary importance in defining the roles and powers of state institutions and in upholding the freedoms to be accorded to individuals. The constitution is built upon principles enshrined in several major statutory sources. Historical examples would include:

⮑ Magna Carta (1215) – this placed limits upon monarchical power and gave protection for liberties to be enjoyed by 'freemen of the realm'. It is now of symbolic importance only.
⮑ The Petition of Right (1628) – this forbade the imposition of loans and taxes by the King without the consent of Parliament.
⮑ Bill of Rights (1689) – this moved the balance of power away from the Crown and provided for the emergence of Parliament as an autonomous and supreme legislature.
⮑ Act of Settlement (1700) – this clarified the line of succession to the throne and gave security of tenure to judges (protected salaries).
⮑ Acts of Union (1536–43, 1707) – these united Wales, England, and subsequently Scotland under one Parliament of Great Britain.

There are a great many more examples that could be included: the Habeas Corpus Act, the Ireland Act, the Reform Acts, the Parliament Acts, the Statute of Westminster – and the list goes on.

The importance of legislation has grown increasingly in modern times, with common law sources being gradually superseded by legislative provisions. The most striking example of this is the Human Rights Act 1998, which has for the first time put the protection of fundamental human rights on a statutory basis. Other recent Acts of major constitutional importance would include the Acts establishing devolution. We will look at these examples in more detail later in this book.

Case law

Parliament's will is supreme in making the law, but it is the judiciary who interpret the law to fit within the constitutional framework. It is through their interpretations of the law, both statutory and common law, and through their powers to review secondary legislation that much of constitutional importance has been decided. It is judicial precedent that provides us with the definition of the relationship between the institutions of the state – the Crown, the executive, Parliament and the judiciary – and the relationship between the state and the individual.

Development of the common law   The development of common law rules by judges has provided much of the fabric of constitutional law. The old case of *Entick v Carrington* (1765) is often quoted as an example. In that case the common law was developed to protect an individual's rights and to restrain exorbitant governmental power. Entick, a critic of the King, had his house raided and private papers removed under a general warrant. The House of Lords ruled that such a warrant was illegal. Lord Camden made it clear that if the Government was to interfere with an individual's rights, it would have to point to specific statutory or common law powers. In these circumstances there were none, and therefore to take personal papers in this manner amounted to a trespass.

Statutory interpretation Judicial input is also made through statutory interpretation. This may be best illustrated by the extent to which judges are willing to interpret legislation in favour of protection for fundamental rights. For example, in *R v Secretary of State for the Home Department ex p Simms and Another* (1999), the Home Secretary had imposed a blanket ban excluding visits to prisoners by journalists for interviews. The policy was found to be unlawful in so far as it interfered with freedom of speech. The House of Lords did not favour the Home Secretary's interpretation of the relevant legislative provision and indicated that in the absence of express language in the legislation, the courts will presume that Parliament's intention is not to infringe the basic rights of the individual. This active protection of fundamental rights has been given added impetus by the enactment of the Human Rights Act 1998. Indeed, examples of subsequent cases, such as *R v A* (2001), suggest that the courts may be even more radical in their interpretations to protect human rights, 'reading down' unambiguous statutory provisions and implying words to ensure compatibility with Convention rights (see Chapter 6).

Judicial review Judicial review provides an important source of case law for the constitution. It is the review of acts, decisions and omissions of public authorities in order to establish whether they have exceeded or abused their powers. As such it is an important factor in limiting the powers of government and state institutions. We will examine judicial review in detail in Chapter 7.

EU law

EU law as a source of constitutional law may be found in:

- treaties;
- regulations; and
- directives.

The European Communities Act 1972 and the subsequent Treaties of the European Union govern the UK's membership of the EU and have great significance for the constitution. By acceding to the EU (formerly the EC), the UK has had to accept the supremacy of EU law. This position raises an obvious conflict with the traditional doctrine of parliamentary sovereignty (see Chapter 2, below). It is important to understand the means of enforcement of EU law, the institutions, and the relationship with domestic law. These matters will be examined in detail in Chapter 3.

The Royal Prerogative

Examples of prerogative powers include:

- the right to prorogue Parliament;
- the right to give assent or dissent to bills;
- the right to appoint the Prime Minister;
- the declaration of war;
- the making of treaties;
- the prerogative of mercy.

The Royal Prerogative as a source of law has its origins in the historical powers of a monarch to act unfettered by Parliament. Today, such powers are now heavily curtailed and it is now accepted that no new prerogative powers can be created (*BBC v Johns* (1965), *per* Diplock LJ). The vast majority of these powers are now exercised by the Government in the name of the Crown. They relate mostly to political rules and, as such, while the courts do rule on the existence and scope of these powers, they are reluctant to interfere with their exercise. These powers are considered more fully in Chapter 2 in the context of the other fundamental concepts underlying the constitution.

Non-legal sources

The non-legal sources of constitutional law are:

- conventions; and
- authoritative textbooks.

Authoritative textbooks

Authoritative texts, such as the writings of Dicey, Blackstone, Jennings and later commentators, are a non-legal source of constitutional law. However, the most important non-legal source is constitutional conventions.

Conventions

Much of the constitution is regulated not by law but by conventions. These unwritten obligations are central to the operation of the constitution: they govern the exercise of discretionary powers and regulate many practices in the workings of central government. In contrast to legal rules, the courts do not enforce these obligations that lie at the heart of the constitution. Hilaire Barnett summarised the meaning of a constitutional convention as:

> a non-legal rule which imposes an obligation on those bound by the convention, breach or violation of which will give rise to legitimate criticism; and that criticism will

generally take the form of an accusation of 'unconstitutional conduct'. (*Constitutional and Administrative Law* (2002))

It may be added that conventions exist to some extent in all constitutions, whether written or unwritten. They are the non-legal rules necessary to regulate the legal rules of a constitution, or, as Sir Ivor Jennings put it, they put flesh on the dry bones of the law.

Examples of conventions are:

Conventions relating to the executive
- the sovereign must not exercise power without advice from the executive,
- the monarch must choose the leader of the majority party in the House of Commons as Prime Minister,
- the Prime Minister and the Chancellor must be members of the House of Commons,
- if a 'vote of confidence' is lost the Government must resign.

Conventions relating to the legislature
- the monarch must assent to Bills passed by the Houses of Parliament,
- the House of Lords must ultimately defer to the Commons,
- money Bills can only be introduced in the Commons and by a Government minister,
- ministers are individually and collectively responsible to Parliament.

Conventions relating to the judiciary
- judges must not be active in party politics,
- MPs shall not criticise the judiciary.

Characteristics of conventions The characteristics of conventions are that:

- they are non-legal – the courts will not enforce them;

- they are evolving;
- they are flexible;
- there is no set sanction for breach.

The uncertainty of conventions It should be noted that conventions change over time, with some falling into disuse and others emerging, and others simply evolving to meet the accepted practices of the day. An example of this flexibility and uncertainty will be seen when we examine the convention of individual ministerial responsibility in Chapter 4. The classic doctrine was that the minister was responsible for every action of his department and that he must answer for any failings. The modern convention has changed to reflect the growth in the size of ministerial departments, and subsequent decisions of ministers have reflected a less wholehearted acceptance of responsibility.

The effect of breaching conventions Conventions are binding only in so far as the participants feel obliged to follow them. While some conventions seem likely never to be breached in modern Britain, such as the convention that the monarch will assent to a Bill duly presented to her by Parliament, other conventions have been broken, and with differing results. For example, collective ministerial responsibility is a convention that requires the inner circle of government to speak with one collective voice publicly on policy and for cabinet ministers not to disclose cabinet discussions. In 1975, the cabinet of the Labour Government was deeply divided over whether or not to continue membership of the European Community. In the circumstance the Prime Minister 'lifted' the convention, allowing cabinet members publicly to advocate their differing views. Upon resolution of the issue, the convention was fully reinstated. No consequences followed from the breach. This illustrates the adaptability of conventions in contrast with the rigidity of laws. A differing consequence of breach occurred when a convention broke down in 1908, when the House of Lords rejected a Finance Bill of the Commons. The then convention required the House of Lords ultimately to give way to the Commons, particularly on financial matters. Legally, at that time the Lords enjoyed equal powers with the Commons. The response to the breach was the enactment of the Parliament Act 1911, restricting the Lords to a power of delay, in effect placing the convention on a statutory basis. In conclusion, there is no hard and fast rule as to what ramification follows from the breach of a convention.

Conventions and the courts   As they are non-legal rules, the courts have no jurisdiction to enforce conventions, though they will recognise their existence. For example, in *Attorney General v Jonathan Cape Ltd* (1976), a cabinet minister sought to publish his diaries revealing cabinet differences, contrary to the convention of collective responsibility (see above). The court recognised the existence and importance of the convention and the constitutional obligation it imposed, but publication could not be prevented simply on the basis that it breached such a convention, as the courts had no powers to enforce conventions. The court did consider other grounds for an injunction within its jurisdiction, namely, breach of confidence coupled with the public interest, but in the circumstances the injunction was refused. However, the important point was the position taken on conventions. Similarly, in *Reference re Amendment of the Constitution of Canada* (1982), the Supreme Court of Canada, in a lengthy consideration of the relationship between law and convention, also recognised the existence of conventions, but also confirmed the courts' inability to enforce them. The court nonetheless highlighted the constitutional importance of conventions:

It should be borne in mind, however, that, while they are not laws, some conventions may be more important than some laws. Their importance depends on that of the value or principle which they are meant to safeguard. Also they form an integral part of the Constitution and the constitutional system ... constitutional conventions plus constitutional law equal the total Constitution of the country.

Should they be codified? A common question for students is to assess the pros and cons of codifying conventions. It is most often argued that codification is undesirable due to the loss of flexibility and the impingement upon the doctrine of separation of powers (see Chapter 2).

Pros	Cons
➲ Certainty ➲ Clearer insight into rules regulating government ➲ Counter criticisms of arcane procedures ➲ Check on discretionary powers of government	➲ Will lose flexibility and dynamic nature ➲ Could stultify the growth of constitution ➲ If jurisdiction given to courts, could impinge upon doctrine of separation of powers

2 Fundamental concepts underlying the constitution

An understanding of the fundamental concepts underlying the constitution and the interplay between them will provide the essential basis for answering the majority of questions posed in public law exams. The fundamental concepts are:

- Rule of law.
- Separation of powers.
- Royal Prerogative.
- Parliamentary sovereignty.

The rule of law

The essence of the rule of law is that is that no man is above the law, and that all individuals should be equal to all others under the law and not subject to arbitrary rule. Moreover, the concept signifies pre-eminent principles that underpin just societies and that ensure the liberty of the individual.

Dicey's rule of law

The concept has had many interpretations in political theory. They have varied depending upon the advocate's political view of the purpose of law and the functions of the state. A student may be asked to identify a common thread in the various interpretations of the concept. A common starting point is the formulation put forward by AV Dicey in *Introduction to the Study of the Law of the Constitution* (1885). He identified the rule of law as having three main aspects or principles:

- … no man is punishable … except for a distinct breach of law established in the ordinary legal manner before the ordinary courts of the land.
- … every man, whatever be his rank or condition, is subject to the ordinary law of the realm and amenable to the jurisdiction of the ordinary tribunals.
- … the general principles of the constitution are with us as the result of judicial decisions determining the rights of private persons …

The first principle

Dicey's first principle requires that governments should only use powers clearly defined by statute or the common law, and that they should be restricted from using arbitrary or discretionary powers to interfere with the liberty of the individual. The classic example of this principle is found in *Entick v Carrington* (1765), where the seizure of personal papers from the home of a critic of the King under a 'general' warrant was ruled unlawful.

The requirements of clarity in the law and freedom from arbitrary rule were expanded upon by Joseph Raz in *The Rule of Law and its Virtue* (1977), where he stated that laws should be publicised, reasonably stable, non-retrospective, non-contradictory, and that the courts should be accessible and staffed by an independent judiciary. Furthermore, in case law one finds that the judiciary will frequently refer to 'the rule of law' in terms of the fair administration of justice.

In modern Britain, the principle that government should be constrained from arbitrary use of its powers is universally accepted. However, it may be argued that Dicey's principle is breached in so far as the extent of government powers is not always clear. Many such powers emerge from legislation, both primary and secondary, that is frequently widely drawn and lacking in precision. In the criminal sphere, one may point to current legislation providing broad and ill-defined prohibitions on an individual's activities, for example, under recent terrorist legislation or under the Criminal Justice and Public Order Act 1994. Furthermore, in contrast to the protections offered to Mr Entick, many wide discretionary powers exist under current legislation for state officials to interfere with an individual's property, for example under s 20(c) of the Taxes Management Act 1970 (entry with warrant to obtain documents): see *R v Inland Revenue Comrs ex p Rossminster Ltd* (1980). It may be argued that Dicey's principle needs to be modified in the light of the requirements of modern government.

The second principle

The second principle is equality of all before the law. In particular, governments and their officials should have no special exemptions or protections from the law and should be subject to the ordinary courts of the land. Dicey was particularly suspicious of the French system of administrative courts that dealt with legal challenges to the government.

This principle may seem difficult to square with the fact that all individuals are not equal in terms of their legal rights and powers. Clearly, certain individuals have additional legal powers or have a particular legal immunity, such as MPs, judges, minors, the police and members of the armed forces. Therefore, the principle may more aptly be described as requiring that 'all should be equally subject to the law, though the law to which some are subject may be different from the law to which others are subject'. The importance of this second principle was underlined in *Re M* (1993). In this case, Kenneth Baker, the then Home Secretary, argued that a mandatory injunction imposed by the court requiring him to procure the return of a deported asylum seeker, was made without jurisdiction on the basis that he was a minister of the

Crown and the Crown had immunity from injunctions under the Crown Proceedings Act 1947. In rejecting these arguments, Lord Templeman held that:

> ... The judiciary enforce the law against individuals, against institutions and against the executive. The judges cannot enforce the law against the Crown as monarch because the Crown as monarch can do no wrong, but judges enforce the law against the Crown as executive and against the individuals who from time to time represent the Crown ... [T]he argument that there is no power to enforce the law by injunction or contempt proceedings against a minister in his official capacity would, if upheld, establish the proposition that the executive obey the law as a matter of grace and not as a matter of necessity, a proposition which would reverse the result of the Civil War.

The growth of administrative law through judicial review, and the creation of statutory tribunals dealing with particular areas of law such as employment law, would also have concerned Dicey. However, one might argue that the judicial review of public authorities is still undertaken by 'ordinary' judges in the 'ordinary' courts of land, albeit subject to different procedures and criteria. Furthermore, the decisions of most statutory tribunals may be challenged in the 'ordinary' courts of appeal.

The third principle

The third principle relates particularly to Britain's unwritten constitution and concerns the protection of individual rights. Dicey argued that the rights of an individual are only securely protected through specific judicial decisions in cases brought before the courts. This reflected Dicey's mistrust of the general protection of such rights offered by a written constitution or a Bill of Rights. His view was that it is only where the courts will enforce a particular constitutional right that it can have value. He argued that the mere presence of a written constitution offered little where governments chose to disregard it.

This principle is the most frequently criticised as being inaccurate and outmoded. Particular criticism is made of Dicey's view that a Bill of Rights was no more than a pious declaration that no one would enforce. While this may have been the case in 1885, Bills of Rights in developed modern democracies provide clear and powerful protection for fundamental rights. Indeed, in Britain the enactment of the Human Rights Act 1998, incorporating the European Convention on Human Rights into domestic law, recognised that the common law on its own provided insufficient protection for fundamental rights. Surely, it is argued, rights are best protected through a combination of judicial decisions and legislation.

Further principles of the rule of law

Some would argue that Dicey's formulation of the rule of law is too limited in that it is concerned only with the legality of powers and their exercise. Other formulations of the concept go further, to include requirements of positive provision for the well-being and dignity of the citizen in society. For example, the Declaration of Delhi 1959 recognised that:

> The rule of law is a dynamic concept, for the expansion and fulfilment of which jurists are primarily responsible and which should be employed not only to safeguard and advance the civil and political rights of the individual in a free society, but also to establish social, economic, educational and cultural conditions under which his legitimate aspirations and dignity may be realised.

The separation of powers

The constitutional jigsaw

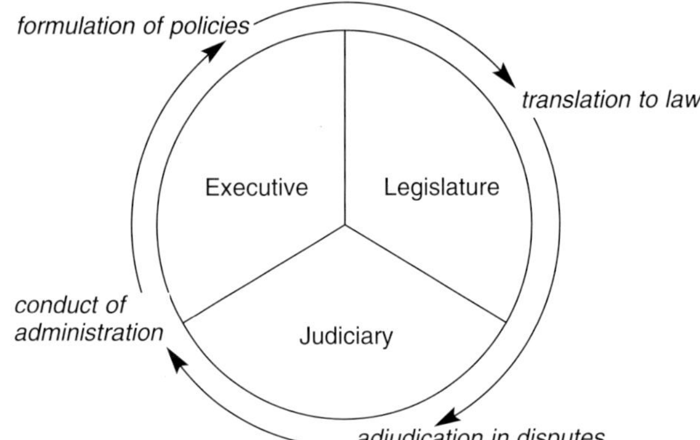

In any state, there are three primary bodies: the executive, the legislature, and the judiciary. The principle of the doctrine of separation of powers is that there should be a clear demarcation in function between each of these bodies, and equally the powers of each should be held in check by the others.

As will be seen, under the constitution of the UK there are important departures from the classic doctrine.

The classic doctrine

The doctrine of separation of powers can be traced back to Aristotle, who proclaimed the virtue of power being distributed between the three primary bodies. However, the classic expression of the necessity for a separation of functions is that of Baron Montesquieu in *De l'Esprit des Lois* (1748):

> When the legislative and executive powers are united in the same person, or in the same body of magistrates, there can be no liberty … Again, there is no liberty if the power of judging is not separated from the legislative and the executive. If it were joined with the legislative, the life and liberty of the subject would be exposed to arbitrary control; for the judge would then be the legislator. If it were joined to the executive power, the judge might behave with violence and oppression. There would be an end to everything if the same man or the same body, whether of the nobles or of the people, were to exercise those three powers, that of enacting laws, that of executing public affairs and that of trying crimes or individual causes.

Montesquieu recognised that in any workable system the separation could not be absolute and that there would be some overlap between the different elements: '… neither should exercise the *whole* power of the other branch of government'. Therefore, his meaning was not that the legislature and the executive should have no influence over each other, but rather that neither should exercise the *whole* power of the other. Montesquieu's doctrine formed the basis for the division of power in the written constitution of the United States. In the US, Congress holds the legislative power and is elected separately from the President. The office of the President holds the executive power: the President and his advisers cannot be members of the Congress. Judicial power is held by the Supreme Court.

The doctrine in the United Kingdom

Fusion of the executive and legislature

The first thing to note in the UK is that there is a near complete fusion of the executive and the legislature. The executive is primarily identified as the Prime Minister and his cabinet. By convention, they must be members of the House of Commons or the House of Lords. This is a clear departure from the doctrine. The Government will of course have a majority in the Commons, and therefore the executive dominates the legislature. This is what led Lord Hailsham to refer to the arrangement as an 'elective dictatorship' (*The Dilemma of Democracy* (1978)). However, supporters of the arrangement point out that it has never led to tyranny. There are many 'checks and balances' in the system, such as the convention of accountability, which requires Government ministers to justify their actions and the actions of their departments to Parliament. The judiciary also exercise control over the use of executive powers by means of judicial review. Ultimately Parliament controls the executive in so far as it can withdraw its support, but where there is a large majority this control may seem illusory. There are also the many procedures for calling the Government to account through questions and debates on the floor of the Houses, and also through the various Select Committees. Lastly, it may be noted that the executive are heavily outnumbered in Parliament: of the 659 MPs, only approximately 100 are Government ministers, including up to 20 who are appointed to the cabinet.

The independence of the judiciary

To a large extent the judiciary form a separate body, for example, judges are barred from becoming members of the House of Commons. In the UK, we seek to achieve the independence of our judiciary by offering them security of tenure under The Act of Settlement 1700. This is elaborated upon in the Supreme Court Act 1981, which provides that judges are removable only in circumstances of serious misbehaviour, and only by Her Majesty on an address presented to her by both Houses of Parliament. In effect senior judges cannot be removed for political reasons.

Furthermore, their salaries are paid from a consolidated fund that is not subject to political control. This independence is to ensure that judges dispense justice according to their judicial oath – 'according to the laws and usage of this realm, without fear or favour, affection or ill-will'.

The legislature and the judiciary

The legislature makes the law, the executive carries it out, and the judiciary interprets and applies it. In its simplest terms, those are the lines of demarcation in the respective functions.

Clearly, under the doctrine of parliamentary sovereignty, the judges cannot question the validity of an Act of Parliament. In other words, they have no power to disregard or reject a statute, even where it is unjust or unpalatable. As Lord Diplock put it:

> Where the meaning of the statutory words are plain and unambiguous it is not for the judges to invent fancied ambiguities as an excuse for failing to give effect to its plain meaning because they themselves consider that the consequences of doing so would be inexpedient, or even unjust or immoral. (*Duport Steels Ltd v Sirs* (1980))

But what if the words are not 'plain and unambiguous'? In such circumstances, Lord Bingham explained:

> The essential function of the court is then to declare the law which it infers that Parliament intended to make, or would have made if it had addressed the point at all. (*The Courts and the Constitution* (1997))

Nevertheless, the senior judges have also stressed that such inferring of Parliament's intention should not extend to judicial legislating. For example, in *Re W and B (Children: Care Plan)* (2002), the Court of Appeal interpreted provisions in the Children Act 1989 to include a duty on local authorities to be subject to 'starred milestones', in other words, that they were required to implement care plans within time limits. There was no such express provision in the legislation. The House of Lords ruled that this interpretation went beyond the boundaries of legitimate interpretation.

The borderline between interpretation and judicial legislating is not always clear, particularly with activist judges such as Lord Denning, who frequently pursued his interpretative role in a highly creative manner. There are added complexities when one considers the interpretative provisions under the European Communities Act 1972 and the Human Rights Act 1998, which provide powerful authority for the courts to interpret legislation to fit with EU law or the European Convention on Human Rights (ECHR). For example, in *R v A* (2001), in order to ensure compatibility with Article 6 ECHR, the House of Lords implied words into a statute that were plainly contrary to Parliament's original intention. We will consider this and other examples of the impact of EU and ECHR law later in the book.

Recent reforms

Historical negations of the doctrine of separation of powers include:

- the position of Lord Chancellor;
- the 'judicial' House of Lords; and
- the appointment of the most senior judges.

The Labour Government has recently addressed a number of these historical negations of the doctrine within the UK constitution. These include the oft-cited example of the office of Lord Chancellor, whose former position as a member of the executive, the legislature and the judiciary was in flagrant breach of the doctrine. The position seemed even more untenable in the light of the Human Rights Act 1998 and the requirements of judicial independence under Article 6 ECHR. Another glaring anomaly is the position of the 'judicial' House of Lords, which sits as a 'committee' within the 'legislative' House of Lords. Lastly, the Government is to address the issue of senior judicial appointments, which previously were made by Her Majesty after consultation with the Prime Minister (following recommendations by the Lord Chancellor).

The initial step in reform was taken in June 2003, when the Prime Minister announced the creation of a new Department for Constitutional Affairs. The department incorporates most of the responsibilities of the former Lord Chancellor's Department, but with new arrangements for judicial appointments and an end to the previous role of the Lord Chancellor as a judge and Speaker of the House of Lords. Once the reforms are confirmed by legislation, the post of Lord Chancellor will be abolished. The Secretary of State for Constitutional Affairs is a conventional cabinet minister and head of department. Further reforms are to include:

- establishment of an independent Judicial Appointments Commission, on a statutory basis, to recommend candidates for appointment as judges;
- creation of a new Supreme Court to replace the existing system of Law Lords operating as a committee of the House of Lords. The new Secretary of State for Constitutional Affairs will not be a member of the Supreme Court;
- reform of the Speakership of the House of Lords. The Speaker will be elected by the Lords themselves and will be independent of the executive, much like the present Speaker in the House of Commons.

The Royal Prerogative

> ... Every act which the executive government can lawfully do without the authority of an Act of Parliament ... (AV Dicey, *Introduction to the Study of the Law of the Constitution* (1885))

Under both written and unwritten constitutions, commonly there exist powers that the executive can exercise without the passage of legislation. Such powers may be referred to as 'inherent executive powers' or 'prerogative powers'. Historically, in Britain, such powers are termed the Royal Prerogative in that they are rooted in the original pre-eminence of the monarchs who could rule and be obeyed in preference to all others.

History

In the early history of the constitution the power of the monarch had very few limitations. Parliament was summoned and dismissed at the monarch's behest, and to a large extent was impotent in controlling his or her prerogative powers. Over the centuries, these powers were gradually eroded. The erosion began with the curbing of the King's powers to impose direct taxes without Parliament's consent. The power of the King to dispense justice and determine cases without judges was rejected in *Prohibitions Del Roy (Case of Prohibitions)* (1607). Similarly, in the *Case of Proclamations* (1611), the court held that the King had no power to proclaim or change the law. The power of the King to raise money for the navy in times of emergency, by indirect taxes and without Parliament's approval, was also denied by the Ship Money Act of 1640, reversing an initial decision of the courts (*Case of Ship Money (R v Hampden)* (1637)). Finally, the Bill of Rights 1689 and the Act of Settlement 1700 curbed the monarch's power as never before. From that time forward, parliamentary sovereignty was established over the Crown and prerogative powers were abolished or curtailed as Parliament determined. Importantly, no new prerogative power could be claimed by the Crown thereafter (see *BBC v Johns* (1965)). Therefore, Royal Prerogative powers are 'the residue of the discretionary or arbitrary authority, which at any time is legally left in the hands of the Crown' (AV Dicey).

The majority of such powers are now exercised by the executive in the name of the Crown, or are exercised by the Crown under the advice of the executive.

Examples of prerogative powers

The following powers are personal to the sovereign:

- the right to appoint the Prime Minister;
- the right to dissolve Parliament;
- the right to give assent or dissent to bills.

The Queen has the power of choosing or dismissing the Prime Minister and deciding whether or not Parliament should be dissolved. In practice the choice of Prime Minister after an election is governed by the convention that the monarch will choose the leader of the party (or coalition of parties) best able to command a majority in the House of Commons. If a Prime Minister resigns through ill-health or old age it may be presumed that the governing party would put forward a new leader to be chosen by the monarch. As to dismissing a Prime Minister, it is inconceivable that a monarch would exercise such a power in modern Britain.

The monarch's power to dissolve Parliament of his or her own volition has not occurred since 1835, and in modern Britain would most likely be regarded as unconstitutional. In practice, it is only on the advice of the Prime Minister that dissolution will take place. By convention, the Prime Minister will seek dissolution if a vote of confidence is lost in the Commons.

By convention, royal assent will be given to those bills duly passed by both Houses of Parliament.

The following powers are exercised by the executive in the name of the Crown:

- the declaration of war;
- the making of treaties;
- the disposition of the armed forces overseas;
- the prerogative of mercy;
- the granting of honours.

The majority of prerogative powers are exercised by the executive in the name of the Crown. The above list is far from exhaustive. In addition, many senior appointments in the armed forces, the security services, the civil service, the judiciary and the Church are made under the Royal Prerogative.

The prerogative power to commit troops to war has come under recent examination in the cases of Sierra Leone, the former Yugoslavia and, most recently, Iraq. In the case of Iraq, the Prime Minister sought and obtained a majority in the House of Commons on the issue of whether or not to commit the troops. In theory, however, the prerogative power could have been exercised without this mandate.

In a discussion document in 2003, the Commons Public Administration Committee advocated that the use of the Royal Prerogative should be investigated by MPs before it actually takes place. However, a Bill that sought to introduce greater parliamentary oversight over the exercise of prerogative powers, the Prime Minister (Office, Role and Functions) Bill 2001, was dropped after the first reading. Thus, the Royal Prerogative remains an important and large, uncontrolled source of powers for the Government.

Judicial control of the prerogative powers

The prerogative as subject to the common law

Regarding judicial review of prerogative powers, the original approach was that the courts could inquire into whether a particular prerogative power existed or not and, if it did exist, they could inquire into its extent. But once the existence and the extent of a power were established, the courts could not inquire into the propriety of its exercise (see *Attorney General v de Keyser's Royal Hotel Ltd* (1920)).

From this early position the courts have gradually shown greater willingness to review the exercise of prerogative powers. In *Chandler v DPP* (1964), it was confirmed that the courts would not review 'the proper exercise of discretionary powers' but, in a new development, they would intervene to correct 'abuse or excess in the exercise of prerogative power'. A more radical change of approach was noted in the landmark case of *R v Criminal Injuries Compensation Board ex p Lain* (1967). The Board had been set up not by statute but by executive action under the prerogative, and on that basis it was argued that it was immune from the review of the courts. The House of Lords rejected that argument, stating that the Board should be subject to review just as if it was set up under statute. The important point made was that the question of whether a particular power was reviewable or not depended not on the source of the power (that is, prerogative power or statute) but on its subject matter. Clearly, it would not be proper for a court to review powers touching on certain subject matters, such as the making of treaties, the defence of the realm, the prerogative of mercy, the grant of honours, the dissolution of Parliament and the appointment of ministers.

This approach was confirmed and amplified in *Council of Civil Service Unions v Minister of State for Civil Service* (the

GCHQ case) (1985). Following a series of disruptive industrial disputes, the Government relied on its prerogative power (an Order in Council) to withdraw the right to union recognition at the government intelligence centre GCHQ. This decision was challenged. Lord Diplock confirmed that administrative decisions taken under prerogative powers are subject to judicial review in the same way as those taken under statutory powers (that is, on the same grounds of 'illegality', 'irrationality' and 'procedural impropriety'). But much as in *ex p Lain* (above), the court recognised that the review of administrative decisions taken under prerogative powers is limited to subject areas that are 'justiciable'. Examples of 'non-justiciable' subject areas would include decisions taken to protect national security. According to Lord Diplock, 'It is par excellence a non-justiciable question. The judicial process is totally inept to deal with the sort of problems which it involves'. In the *GCHQ* case, the House of Lords decided that the evidence of possible dangers to national security outweighed any legitimate expectations of the employees, and the Government's right to determine the terms and conditions of employment was therefore lawfully within its prerogative powers.

Statute and the prerogative

In a number of cases the courts have made clear that where a statute is enacted to regulate a matter previously falling under the prerogative but not expressly abolishing the prerogative, the statute will prevail. In *Attorney General v de Keyser's Royal Hotel Ltd* (1920), the owners of the hotel claimed compensation for war-time damage pursuant to the Defence of the Realm Act 1914. The House of Lords ruled that the Government's decision to award a lesser discretionary sum under prerogative powers was unlawful; the statutory provision had superseded the prerogative power. However, their Lordships made clear that the Government could choose to repeal the statute, such that the prerogative powers would again come into operation, or else the Government might enact new legislation to provide for awards of a lesser amount. This is what occurred following the case of *R v Secretary of State for the Home Department ex p Fire Brigades Union* (1995), where the court had ruled unlawful the decision of the Secretary of State not to implement a statutory scheme of compensation for victims of violence in favour of a scheme providing lesser payments. In response, the Criminal Injuries Compensation Act 1995 repealed the previous statutory scheme and provided for payments in accordance with the scheme preferred by the Secretary of State.

Parliamentary sovereignty

Historically, the rise of parliamentary sovereignty coincided with the gradual erosion of the prerogative powers of the Crown. As we have seen, by the end of the 17th century the powers of the Crown had been reduced to a residue. The Bill of Rights 1688 and the Act of Settlement 1700 declared Parliament as the supreme law-making body. Thereafter, no new law could be enacted without the consent of both Houses of Parliament.

AV Dicey

The classical definition of parliamentary sovereignty in relation to the UK Parliament is provided by AV Dicey:

> The principle of parliamentary sovereignty means neither more nor less than this, namely, that Parliament thus defined has, under the English constitution, the right to make or unmake any law whatever; and, further, that no

person or body is recognized by the law of England as having the right to override or set aside the legislation of Parliament. (*The Law of the Constitution* (1885))

Legal and political limits

At the outset it is important to point that out that Dicey's description of parliamentary sovereignty is concerned only with the *legal limits* of Parliament's powers and should not be confused with the question of whether there are *political or moral limits* to Parliament's powers. For example, a Parliament may be legally capable of repealing the right of women to vote, or enacting laws that require all blue-eyed babies in France to be put to death, but of course politically it is impossible that such laws could be passed – any government is ultimately dependent on its electoral mandate. Nevertheless, the fact that Parliament would not pass abhorrent or electorally unpopular legislation has no bearing upon what it is *legally entitled* to do. In Dicey's view, legal sovereignty was held by the 'Queen in Parliament', while political sovereignty was vested in the people.

Legal sovereignty

From Dicey, we can deduce the doctrine of parliamentary sovereignty in its legal sense to have three elements:

- Parliament is competent to legislate on any matter.
- No Parliament can bind future Parliaments or be bound by its predecessors.
- No court or other person can pass judgment upon the validity of Parliament's legislation.

Competence to legislate on any matter

Parliament's omnicompetence has been traditionally demonstrated by first pointing to its ability to determine its own length and composition. In effect, Parliament is its own master and is subordinate to no other. For example: the Septennial Act 1715 and the Prolongation of Parliament Act 1944 extended the life of a Parliament; the Parliament Acts 1911 and 1949 curtailed the powers of the House of Lords; and the House of Lords Act 1999 altered the composition of the House of Lords.

Furthermore, in case law we find no instance of the courts seeking to review Parliament's right to legislate, even if in breach of international law (*Cheney v Conn* (1968)), or when introducing retrospective legislation (War Damages Act 1965), or when legislating extraterrestrially (War Crimes Act 1991), all areas in which one would intuitively seek limits, if there are any, to Parliament's sovereign powers.

Another area that raises questions is devolution. For example, does the Scotland Act 1998, which devolved substantial legislative powers, divest Westminster of its competence to legislate in those areas? The answer to this in the legal sense is clearly 'No'. In fact, the Act expressly provides that it 'does not affect the power of the Parliament of the UK to make laws for Scotland' (s 28(7)). Whatever the political inhibitions, there is nothing in the act of devolution that invalidates the UK Parliament's right to legislate on any matter.

In *British Coal Corporation v The King* (1935), the Privy Council considered the position where independence was granted to a dominion, here Canada, under the Statute of Westminster 1931. The court recognised that the power of the Imperial Parliament remained 'in theory unimpaired' and, in theory, the granting of independence could be reversed. Of course politically this will never occur, but again the case recognises there are no *legal* limits to Parliament's competency.

No Parliament can bind future Parliaments or be bound by its predecessors

It is this aspect of Dicey's definition that gives rise to the most debate. The orthodox view is that no Parliament can enact rules that limit future Parliaments. In other words, there is no means of entrenching or protecting legislation such that future Parliaments will be bound. The Acts of Union, the Human Rights Act and the European Communities Act have no greater legal status or protection from repeal than the Vinegar Act (repealed) had.

Express and implied repeal

Parliament may enact a law that expressly repeals any previous law, and the courts must give effect to the latter provision (*express repeal*). Where Parliament enacts a law that does not expressly repeal an earlier statute but is in conflict with it, the courts will follow the latest statute in time under the doctrine of *implied repeal* of the earlier statute. Furthermore, in two cases, *Vauxhall Estates Ltd v Liverpool Corporation* (1932) and *Ellen Street Estates Ltd v Minister of Health* (1934), the court considered a statute (Acquisition of Land (Assessment of Compensation) Act 1919) that expressly excluded the doctrine of implied repeal, providing that any conflicting provisions of later statutes should have no effect. The later Housing Act 1925 provided lesser, and therefore conflicting, provisions for compensation. The court held that the exclusion of the doctrine of implied repeal under the 1919 Act could have no effect because 'the legislature cannot, according to our constitution, bind itself as to the form of subsequent legislation', and therefore the provisions of the later Act were applied.

However, the position is not completely certain. Some constitutional theorists argue that Parliament could prescribe special procedures for passing future legislation that could be made binding on future Parliaments. They rely on the Privy Council decision in *Attorney General for New South Wales v Trethowan* (1932). In 1929, the outgoing government of NSW, through its majority in Parliament, enacted legislation providing that the legislative ('upper') chamber could not be abolished without a two-thirds majority in both chambers and the support of a public referendum. In 1930, the incoming government sought to repeal the protective legislation and abolish the upper chamber without regard to its provisions. The Privy Council held that the later Parliament was bound by the 'manner and form' requirements of the earlier legislation. The judgment referred to s 5 of the Colonial Laws Validity Act 1865, which provides that the legislature of NSW had full powers to legislate for its own constitution, but also expressly provides that it may prescribe the manner and form in which laws are passed.

There is no equivalent example in the UK and the orthodox view is that the *Trethowan* case is irrelevant here since, unlike the 'subordinate' NSW legislature, the UK Parliament is sovereign and its powers are not derived from any statute. Nonetheless, it may be noted, there is nothing to prevent Parliament from creating special procedures to be followed before legislation is passed. For example, s 1 of the Northern Ireland Act 1998 provides that any legislation to remove Northern Ireland from the UK would require the holding of a prior referendum. However, under the UK constitution this guarantee of a referendum provided by the 1998 Act could be repealed by subsequent legislation. We again return to the difference between what a legislature is legally entitled to do and what would be politically acceptable.

No court or other person can pass judgment upon the validity of Parliament's legislation

The legislature makes the law and the courts apply it. Underlying the doctrine of parliamentary sovereignty is the rule that the courts will not question the validity of an Act of Parliament. This rule is not defined in any statute, and in this sense the doctrine is rooted in the common law, as it is the judges who uphold Parliament's sovereignty by obeying the rule:

> ... the duty of the court is to obey and apply every Act of Parliament, and ... the court cannot hold any such Act to be *ultra vires*. Of course there may be questions about what the Act means, and of course there is power to hold statutory instruments and other subordinate legislation *ultra vires*. But once an instrument is recognised as being an Act of Parliament, no English court can refuse to obey it or question its validity. (*Manuel v AG* (1983), *per* Megarry VC)

The position may be contrasted with the powers of the Supreme Court in the US, which has the power to decide whether or not legislation conforms to the US constitution.

Perhaps the most common issue in this area for students to consider is the impact of both EU law and the Human Rights Act 1998 on Dicey's third principle.

European Communities Act 1972 The impact of European law on parliamentary sovereignty is always a topical issue for students. The European Communities Act 1972, s 2(4) provides that 'any enactment passed or to be passed ... shall be construed and have effect subject to the foregoing provisions of this section'. The 'foregoing provisions' are those in s 2(1) of the Act giving effect in the UK to directly effective EU law. In effect, directly effective EU law takes precedence over a domestic statute.

In applying these provisions, the courts have sometimes had to strain the meaning of statutory words, or read non-existent words into a statutory provision, in order to give effect to superseding EU law. Usually, this will be contrary to Parliament's original intention. However, the use of *constructive* or *purposive statutory interpretation* in this manner is said not to be contrary to the doctrine of parliamentary sovereignty in as much as the courts are but implementing Parliament's will under the 1972 Act (*Macarthys v Smith* (1981), *per* Lord Denning MR).

On occasion a statute will be so baldly inconsistent with directly effective EU law that the court will be unable to construe a compatible interpretation. Controversially, in such circumstances the inconsistent provisions of that statute must be 'disapplied' by the court (*R v Secretary of State for Transport ex p Factortame* (1990)). Plainly, this would appear contrary to Dicey's third principle. However, once again the concept of parliamentary sovereignty is said to remain undisturbed, since the court is simply fulfilling Parliament's intention under the 1972 Act to legislate compatibly and, furthermore, it is always available to Parliament to repeal the 1972 Act outright. If the European Communities Act 1972 was repealed, the 'disapplied provision' would return again to full force and there would be no basis for the courts to question its validity. This and other aspects of European law are considered in detail in the next chapter.

Human Rights Act 1998   After much debate during the passage of the Bill regarding the impact on parliamentary sovereignty, the Government decided not to include in the Human Rights Act (HRA) 1998 any power to disapply or strike down primary legislation. In dismissing the approach under the European Communities Act 1972, the Government differentiated between the UK's 'absolute' obligations under

EU law as opposed to those under the ECHR. Furthermore, ECHR law is not directly effective in the manner of EU law.

Consequently, the powers of the court under the 1998 Act are described as 'interpretative only'. Section 3(1) of the HRA 1998 provides a 'rule of construction' to apply to past as well as future legislation:

> So far as it is possible to do so, primary legislation and subordinate legislation must be read and given effect in a way which is compatible with the Convention rights.

We may contrast the limited obligation in the statutory words of s 3 of the HRA 1998 – 'So far as it is possible to do so ...' – with the total obligation in s 2 of the European Communities Act 1972 – '... shall be construed ...' (see above). Lord Irvine (the then Lord Chancellor) explained the interaction of ss 3 and 4 of the HRA 1998 in the House of Lords:

> Section 3(1) requires legislation to be read and given effect to so far as is possible to do so in a way that is compatible with Convention rights. Section 3(2) provides that where it is not possible to do so ... that does not affect its validity, continuing operation or enforcement. This ensures the courts are not empowered to strike down Acts of Parliament which they find to be incompatible with Convention rights. Instead section 4 of the [Act] ... introduces a new mechanism through which the courts can signal to the Government that a provision of legislation is, in their view, incompatible. It is then for government and Parliament to consider what action should be taken.

Thus sovereignty is very much maintained intact. A declaration of incompatibility may put political pressure on a Government to change the law, but it does not impose any legal duty to do so. Further details of the impact of the HRA 1998 are examined in Chapter 6.

3 The European Union

European integration

European integration is based on four founding treaties:

- Treaty establishing the European Coal and Steel Community (ECSC), which was signed in Paris in 1951. The original members were Germany, France, Belgium, Italy, Luxembourg and The Netherlands.
- Treaty establishing the European Economic Community (EEC).
- Treaty establishing the European Atomic Energy Community (Euratom), which was signed (along with the EEC Treaty) in Rome in 1957.
- Treaty on European Union, which was signed in Maastricht in 1992, organising the newly named 'European Union' into three 'pillars'. The most important pillar is that of the European Community (replacing the EEC) which is governed by Community law. The second pillar provides for common areas of foreign and security policy. The third pillar provides for common areas on justice and home affairs. The second and third pillars are not governed by Community law but are achieved through intergovernmental co-operation.

Three pillars of the European Union

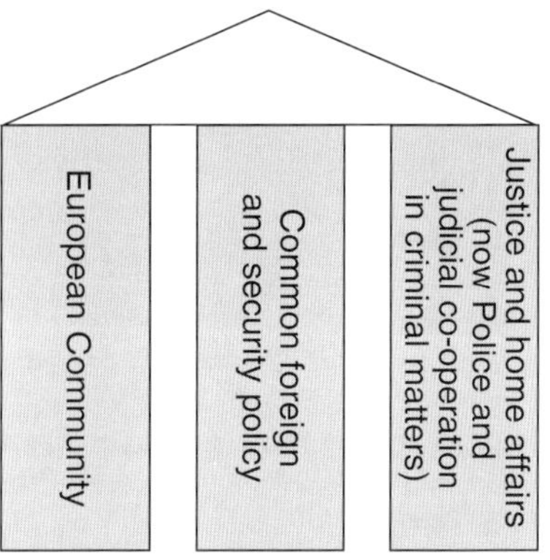

The founding treaties have been amended on several occasions, particularly following the accession of new Member States. The United Kingdom acceded in 1973. Other major treaties include the following:

⇨ The Merger Treaty 1965 merged the then three European Communities under a single set of institutions. The 'institutional triangle' now consists of the Commission, the Council and Parliament, and these are flanked by two more institutions – the Court of Justice and the Court of Auditors.

⇨ The Single European Act 1986 (a European treaty, not a domestic Act) set out a timetable for the removal of all barriers to trade between the Member States, and to turn the 'common market' into a genuine single market in which goods, services, people and capital could move around freely. The Single Market was formally completed at the end of 1992.

○ The Treaty of Amsterdam 1997 amended and renumbered the Articles of the EU and EC Treaties. One of the main purposes of this Treaty was to simplify the decision-making procedures within the European Union. The Treaty substantially boosted the elected European Parliament's supervisory powers over the Commission. The European Parliament now must approve the appointment of the Commission, which has been the subject of its criticisms. The Treaty also extends the areas in which decisions can be taken by a qualified majority, and encourages closer ties with national parliaments. One development has occasioned considerable debate, whereby Member States that intend to establish closer co-operation may make use of the institutions, procedures and mechanisms laid down in the Treaties, subject to the provisos specified. This ultimately opens the way for a multi-speed Europe, albeit with limitations.

○ A single European currency managed by a European Central Bank was introduced in 1999. The single currency – the euro – became a reality on 1 January 2002, when euro notes and coins replaced national currencies in 12 of the then 15 countries of the European Union. The United Kingdom has continued to exercise its 'opt-out'.

○ The Treaty of Nice 2001 was primarily concerned with preparation for the enlargement of the EU. A consolidated version of both the EU and EC Treaties was adopted. In a declaration of the future of the Union at Nice, it was stated that the following issues needed to be addressed in the lead up to the next intergovernmental conference in 2004: a more precise delimitation of powers between Union and Member States; the status of the Charter of Fundamental Rights; simplification of the Treaties; and the role of national parliaments in the European system.

⮑ Further changes will result from the activities of the Convention on the Future of Europe chaired by Giscard d'Estaing. The duty of the members of the Convention is to write a Constitution for Europe. A draft has already been presented. Major changes will also ensue from the Treaty on the Accession of 10 new Member States, which was signed in April 2003 and enters into force on 1 May 2004.

Legal doctrines of EU law

⮑ Attribution of powers.
⮑ Subsidiarity.
⮑ Proportionality.

Article 5 (as inserted by the Maastricht Treaty 1992) of the EC Treaty provides three central legal principles:

[1] The Community shall act within the limits of the powers conferred upon it by this Treaty and of the objectives assigned to it therein.

[2] In areas which do not fall within its exclusive competence, the Community shall take action, in accordance with the principle of subsidiarity, only if and in so far as the objectives of the proposed action cannot be sufficiently achieved by the Member States and can therefore, by reason of the scale or effects of the proposed action, be better achieved by the Community.

[3] Any action by the Community shall not go beyond what is necessary to achieve the objectives of this Treaty.

Attribution of powers

The principle of attribution of powers, contained within the first sentence of the Article, provides that the Community is entitled to act only when it is given the express power to do so.

Subsidiarity

The principle of attribution of powers is supplemented by the key concept of subsidiarity. According to this concept, as it may be understood in its strict legal sense, the Community not only has to show that it has the power to act, but must also justify why it and not the Member State should act. There is, however, an important qualification on the operation of this principle, in that it cannot be applied to matters falling within the Community's exclusive competence, sometimes referred to as the *occupied field*. In short, it is intended to operate only in relation to those areas where the Community has a parallel competence with Member States.

Proportionality

The third principle, that of proportionality, as expressed in the last sentence of Article 5, applies not only to areas of parallel competence, but also to areas of exclusive competence. It requires that the measure of Community action must be in proportion to the objective being pursued.

Examples of competences in EU law are shown the diagram below.

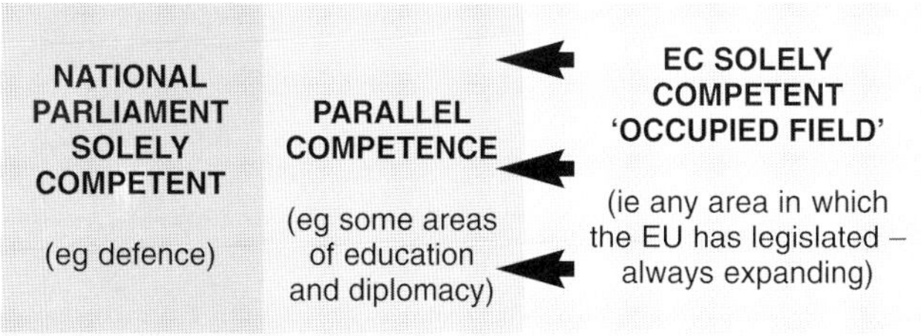

Sources of Community law

➲ Primary sources
- The Treaties as amended

➲ Secondary sources
- Regulations
- Directives

➲ Other sources
- Recommendations and Opinions
- Decisions of the European Court of Justice (ECJ)

Article 249 of the EC Treaty defines the different types of legislation:

> A regulation shall have general application. It shall be binding in its entirety and directly applicable in all Member States.

> A directive shall be binding, as to the result to be achieved, upon each Member State to which it is addressed, but shall leave to the national authorities the choice of form and methods.

> A decision shall be binding in its entirety upon those to whom it is addressed.

> Recommendations and opinions shall have no binding force.

Therefore, only regulations, directives and decisions (and of course Treaty Articles) are legally binding, and only these can create rights on which individuals may rely before a national court or before the ECJ. Treaty Articles and regulations are directly applicable, in other words they become part of the domestic law of Member States without any implementing action being taken, whereas directives require implementation by domestic legislation.

The ECJ is the final arbiter on Community law. Under Article 234, national courts may seek a preliminary ruling from the ECJ on matters of Community law relevant to the case before them.

Supremacy of EC law

The supremacy of EC law is a doctrine that has been developed by the ECJ: there is no express provision in the Treaty as to whether Community law or national law is to have priority.

In *Costa v Enel* (1964), the ECJ stated that the EEC Treaty, unlike any ordinary treaty, created a legal system that by virtue of accession became integral to the legal systems of the Member States. Furthermore, by entering into the Treaty, the Member States had limited their sovereignty, in so far as the national courts were bound to apply EC law in preference to conflicting domestic legislation.

In the *Simmenthal* case (1978), it was further clarified that every national court must

> apply Community law in its entirety and protect rights which the latter confers on individuals and must accordingly set aside any provision of national law which may conflict with it, whether prior or subsequent to the Community rule.

Supremacy of EC law in the UK

In the UK there is a *dualist* approach to international law, which means that international law cannot become part of the domestic legal system until it is incorporated by an Act of Parliament. Therefore, in order for Community law to become part of the UK's domestic law, it had to be incorporated by the European Communities Act (ECA) 1972.

Section 2(1) of the ECA 1972 provides that directly applicable EC law is given effect without the need for further domestic legislation. Section 2(2) provides for the making of delegated legislation in order to implement EC obligations that would not otherwise be directly applicable. Section 2(4) provides that all subsequent UK legislation is to be construed and have effect subject to the provisions of s 2(1) and (2). Section 3 instructs the courts to decide any issues of Community law 'in accordance with the principles laid down by ... the European Court'. The 1972 Act therefore appeared to give effect to the supremacy of EC law.

However, doubts still remained as to what would actually happen if a domestic Act were passed after 1972 containing provisions inconsistent with Community law. Would s 2(4) of the ECA 1972 prevail and the conflicting domestic legislation be set aside? How could this be squared with parliamentary sovereignty?

Possible conflict with parliamentary sovereignty

As we saw in Chapter 2, the traditional view of sovereignty as advanced by Dicey is that Parliament is omnicompetent, and that no Act of Parliament will be invalidated by the courts. Furthermore, it is always open to Parliament to repeal any previous legislation, and that in the case of conflict between two Acts of Parliament, the later repeals the earlier, and that therefore no Parliament could bind its successors. In short, there is no means for the entrenchment of legislation. Did this mean that the ECA 1972 was subject to the doctrine of 'implied repeal'? For example, would the provision in s 2(4) of that Act that 'any enactment ... shall be construed and have effect subject to [Community law]' be overridden by subsequent inconsistent legislation? Clearly, if it were overridden, that would not be consistent with the supremacy of EC law as expressed in *Costa v Enel* (1964).

The courts managed for many years to avoid the issue of a direct confrontation between EC law and domestic law, through the use of strong principles of statutory interpretation. Lord Denning MR explained the basis of this approach in *Macarthys v Smith* (1979):

> In construing our statute, we are entitled to look to the Treaty as an aid to its construction; but not only as an aid but as an overriding force. If on close investigation it should appear that our legislation is deficient or is inconsistent with Community law by some oversight of our draftsmen then it is our bounden duty to give priority to Community law. Such is the result of s 2(1) and (4) of the ECA 1972.

Examples of such an approach include *Garland v British Rail* (1983), where a literal interpretation of a provision of the Sex Discrimination Act 1975 appeared inconsistent with Article 141 (then Article 119) EC (equal pay). However, the House of Lords was able to construe the provision in a manner consistent with the Article. This *purposive approach* to interpretation was taken further in the cases of *Pickstone v Freemans plc* (1989) and *Litster v Forth Dry Dock* (1990), where additional words were implied into domestic legislative provisions to ensure compatibility with Community law. However, it may be noted that Lord Denning MR in *Macarthys* did go on to state that if Parliament deliberately passed an Act with the intention of negating a provision of the Treaty, the courts would have to follow the statute.

The leading case in the UK on the question of sovereignty is *R v Secretary of State for Transport ex p Factortame Ltd (No 2)* (1991), which involved a direct conflict between UK legislation and Community law in a dispute involving fishing rights. The Merchant Shipping Act 1988 and its subordinate legislation sought to limit the extent to which foreign nationals could register as British vessel owners in order to prevent what was called 'quota hopping'. The provisions were challenged on the basis that they were in breach of Community law on a number of grounds, most obviously that they discriminated between EU citizens on the basis of nationality.

First, the House of Lords ruled that where it was established by the ECJ that a provision of domestic law was in breach of Community law, the provisions of Community law would prevail. On a further question of whether, pending a decision of the ECJ on the issue of breach, a national court could set aside domestic legislation by way of interim relief, the House of Lords ruled (reversing an earlier decision) that it could. The latter part of the decision followed a ruling of the ECJ that required national courts to set aside domestic legislation in such circumstances as existed in this case, namely, where the applicants would otherwise suffer very severe and irrecoverable damage.

On the question of sovereignty, Lord Bridge had this to say:

> Some public comments on the decision of the Court of Justice, affirming the jurisdiction of the courts of the Member States to override national legislation if necessary to enable interim relief to be granted in protection of rights under Community law, have suggested that this was a novel and dangerous invasion by a Community institution of the sovereignty of the United Kingdom Parliament. But such comments are based on a misconception. If the supremacy within the European Community of Community law over the national law of Member States was not always inherent in the EEC Treaty it was certainly well established in the jurisprudence of the Court of Justice long before the United Kingdom joined the Community. Thus, whatever limitation of its sovereignty Parliament accepted when it enacted the European Communities Act 1972 was entirely voluntary. Under the terms of the 1972 Act it has always

been clear that it was the duty of a United Kingdom court, when delivering final judgment, to override any rule of national law found to be in conflict with any directly enforceable rule of Community law. Similarly, when decisions of the Court of Justice have exposed areas of United Kingdom statute law which failed to implement Council directives, Parliament has always loyally accepted the obligation to make appropriate and prompt amendments. Thus there is nothing in any way novel in according supremacy to rules of Community law in areas to which they apply and to insist that, in the protection of rights under Community law, national courts must not be prohibited by rules of national law from granting interim relief in appropriate cases is no more than a logical recognition of that supremacy.

Conclusion

In summary we may say that the doctrine of *implied repeal*, under which inconsistencies between later and earlier legislation are resolved in favour of the later legislation, does not apply to clashes concerning Community and national law. If Parliament ever does wish to derogate from its Community obligations then it will have to do so *expressly and unequivocally*. The reaction of our national courts to such an unlikely eventuality remains to be seen. (See further P Craig, *EU Law and National Constitutions: The UK* (2003).)

Lastly, it is argued that parliamentary sovereignty is maintained by the very fact that any UK Parliament has the legal power to repeal the ECA 1972. If it did so the constraints of Community law would be removed and all previously 'disapplied' legislation, such as the Merchant Shipping Act 1988, would return into full force. However, except in the unlikely event of repeal of the ECA 1972, the supremacy of EU law over domestic law will remain of fundamental constitutional importance.

4 The executive

Introduction

While we primarily identify the executive as the Prime Minister and his chosen Government ministers, the personnel of the executive in fact includes the staff of all Government departments and all civil servants. The primary functions of the executive are to execute and formulate policies and to implement legislation. Beyond Government departments, the civil service undertakes the day-to-day administration of executive powers, such as the police force, which administers law and order, or the army, which undertakes the defence of the nation. However, in this chapter we shall use the term 'the executive' in its particular sense, that is, to refer to those members of central Government holding executive power.

Central Government

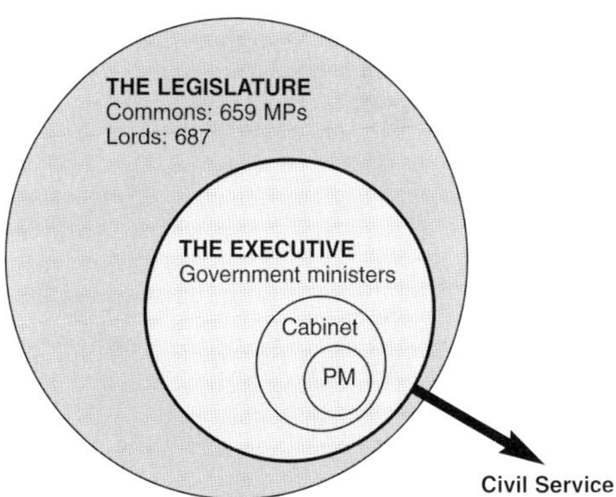

Appointment and powers of the Prime Minister

The appointment of the Prime Minister is by the monarch according to the convention that the monarch must appoint the MP who is best able to command a stable majority. Once appointed, the Prime Minister will appoint his cabinet. Constitutionally, the monarch makes the appointments to the cabinet on the advice of the Prime Minister. The Prime Minister also chooses which Government departments should be represented in cabinet, though certain ministers, such as the Chancellor of the Exchequer, the Foreign Secretary and the Home Secretary, will always hold a seat in cabinet. The recent creation of a Department of Constitutional Affairs and the discontinuance of the Lord Chancellor's Department demonstrate the extent of the Prime Minister's powers in this regard. It is also for the Prime Minister to decide whether cabinet members should remain in office.

Origins of the cabinet

The origins of cabinet government lie in the17th century and the creation, by King Charles II, of a small cabal of privy counsellors in order to alleviate the frustration of working through the full Privy Council. Thus, far from being created by statute, the cabinet merely evolved out of the Privy Council and is still technically one of its committees. At first, the members of the cabinet were important court officials and not responsible to Parliament. However, in the 18th century, parliamentary power steadily increased and it became politically expedient for the monarch to choose as close advisers politicians with sufficient influence in Parliament to secure the passage of measures, and especially financial measures, through the legislature.

By the time of the Reform Acts of 1832 and 1867, the power of the monarch to appoint ministers without taking the advice of leading parliamentary figures was effectively lost. With the expansion in the electorate came a growth in party politics. The cabinet then began to emerge as the dominant political body within the constitution, representing in government the collective leadership of the party that was able to command a majority in the House of Commons.

From this growing dominance of the cabinet emerged two conventions of the constitution, which are crucial to the working of modern cabinet government. The first is that ministers of the Crown are accountable, both collectively and individually, to Parliament; the second, that the Crown must act only as ministers advise it to act.

Out of the prominent party figures within the cabinet, it was inevitable that a leading figure would be recognised. It is from this that the office of Prime Minister evolved. Thus, as with the cabinet, its existence and powers are defined only by convention.

Exercise of executive power

Cabinet government

As the central decision-making body, the cabinet holds great power. We noted in Chapter 2 that there is a near complete fusion of the executive and legislature, such that the executive in effect now dominates the legislature. Lord Hailsham examined the progressive growth of executive power when he delivered The Dimbleby Lecture, entitled 'Elective dictatorship', in 1972. Lord Hailsham traced the movement within our constitution from medieval monarchy to modern democracy, and noted:

> There has been a continuous enlargement of the scale and range of Government itself. The checks and balances, which in practice used to prevent abuse, have now disappeared. ... Until comparatively recently Parliament consisted of two effective Chambers. Now for most

practical purposes, it consists of one. Until recently, the power of the Government within Parliament was largely controlled either by the Opposition or by its own Backbenchers. It is now largely in the hands of the Government machine. Until recently, debate and argument dominated the Parliamentary scene. Now, it is the whips and the Party Caucus ... Debate is becoming a ritual dance, sometimes interspersed with catcalls.

Prime ministerial government?

A lot of recent debate surrounds the relationship between the Prime Minister and the cabinet, and has focused on the apparent dominance of the Prime Minister over cabinet colleagues. It is argued that, having moved from parliamentary government to cabinet government, we have now moved to prime ministerial government. Supporting such a view, ex-cabinet members such as Mo Mowlam and Claire Short have expressed frustration at the side-lining of the cabinet, arguing that the Prime Minister has become increasingly presidential, and that the role of cabinet has been replaced by an inner coterie of unelected advisers. However, commentators such as Peter Hennessy, in *The Prime Minister: The Office and its Holders since 1945* (2001), concludes that the extent of prime ministerial dominance will depend very much upon the individual personality of the incumbent Prime Minister and that broad generalisations should not be drawn. Furthermore, he submits that little has changed in recent times, in that the Prime Minister is still ultimately dependent on the consensus of his cabinet and his party to remain in office. The resignation of Margaret Thatcher in 1990 reveals how even a powerful Prime Minister can lose office through the loss of support amongst her cabinet.

Ministerial responsibility

There are two central conventions under the constitution to ensure the executive's accountability to Parliament, and ultimately to the electorate:

- Collective ministerial responsibility.
- Individual ministerial responsibility.

Collective responsibility

- Government must speak with one voice.
- Cabinet discussions are confidential.
- The Government must resign if it loses a 'confidence vote'.

Government must speak with one voice/confidentiality

The underlying rationale to this convention and the convention of confidentiality is the need for the Government to present a united front. The classic expression of the importance of collective responsibility in this regard remains that of Lord Salisbury:

> For all that passes in Cabinet, every member of it who does not resign is absolutely and irretrievably responsible … It is only on the principle that absolute responsibility is undertaken by every member of the Cabinet, who, after a decision is arrived at remains a member of it, that the joint responsibilities of Ministers to Parliament can be upheld and one of the essential responsibilities of parliamentary responsibility established. (Official Report, HC, 1878)

At basis, all members of the cabinet must accept and publicly defend decisions made in cabinet, or else resign. Furthermore, the convention of confidentiality allows members of the cabinet to discuss things freely, in the knowledge that any disagreement will be protected from the public gaze. On occasions the convention of presenting a united front has been suspended, most notably in 1975 for the period of the referendum on continuing European Community membership, where cabinet members were permitted to campaign on either side. More recently, the Major Government 'agreed to differ' on the single currency issue, uniting under the agreed 'wait and see' formula.

It may be noted that owing to the modern expansion of government and in order to relieve the pressure on the full cabinet, most decisions are not made in cabinet but in smaller cabinet committees. There are both permanent and *ad hoc* committees, and nowadays they constitute the heart of Government policy-making. The Prime Minister determines the identity and composition of these cabinet committees, and most are chaired by leading members of the cabinet. The convention of collective responsibility equally applies to these committees, in that their recommendations must, in normal circumstances, be accepted by the cabinet. This extension of the principle of collective responsibility has been criticised, in that members of the cabinet will frequently not be party to the decision made by a cabinet committee. For example, Michael Heseltine resigned in 1986 following a decision made by a cabinet committee on the future of the Westland Helicopter company, and after Margaret Thatcher had refused to have the matter discussed in the full cabinet.

Confidence rule

A Government must resign if it loses the support of the elected chamber. The principle is that where a confidence vote is tabled and lost by the Government, the Prime Minister must resign and seek the dissolution of Parliament. The convention is of crucial significance to the operation of the UK constitution. It goes to the very heart of the relationship between the executive and the legislature. Some would argue that it is too unwieldy a power for Parliament to use effectively, in so far as it is an 'all or nothing' decision to support or not to support; nonetheless, it is the ultimate guarantee that the executive acts with the authority of Parliament.

The convention can actually serve to strengthen the position of the executive. Thus, when John Major and his cabinet suffered a defeat in Parliament in July 1992 on a motion relating to the Maastricht Treaty on European Union (largely at the hands of backbench 'euro-sceptic' rebels), he was able to restore his authority by putting down a motion of confidence for the following day. The motion inevitably secured a majority, as the rebels within his party knew that its defeat would have led to the dissolution of Parliament and the possibility of the Labour Party winning the ensuing general election.

Individual ministerial responsibility

On a day-to-day level much of the administration of executive powers and policies is carried out by the civil service, both in government departments and more widely in the provision of public services. How is the exercise of these powers to be made accountable to Parliament? One of the important features of the civil service is its claim to political neutrality. In particular, civil servants in government departments are meant to remain as the anonymous 'advisers' of government ministers. It is felt that without such anonymity their position of permanency within our constitution would be threatened.

To protect this position of anonymity and neutrality, ministers are expected to take responsibility for the civil servants under them. Therefore, ministers are not only responsible to Parliament in a collective sense for the policies of the Government as a whole, but are also responsible in an individual sense for their own actions and those of their departments. In effect, ministers stand as the link between the civil service and Parliament. They will do so by answering parliamentary questions, by introducing and defending Bills, by participating in debates in Parliament and by appearing before Select Committees (see Chapter 5, below).

But are ministers constitutionally responsible for every action undertaken by their civil servants, and what does accepting responsibility entail? The question was central to what has become known as the 'Crichel Down Affair'. In 1939, the Air Ministry compulsorily acquired Crichel Down, an area of farmland in Dorset. After World War II, the land was transferred to the Ministry of Agriculture, which refused a request from the original owners to repurchase it. This refusal was accompanied by misleading replies and the matter was taken up in Parliament. In 1954, following an inquiry which found 'inefficiency, bias and bad faith' on the part of some officials, the minister, Sir Thomas Dugdale, accepted responsibility and resigned.

The most important constitutional aspect of this affair is the subsequent statement by the Home Secretary, Sir David Maxwell-Fyfe, in the House of Commons, on the question of when ministers must accept responsibility for the actions of their civil servants. The Home Secretary made it clear that such a constitutional duty existed where the civil servant was carrying out either Government policy or the explicit orders of the minister. If a civil servant caused delay or made a mistake, but not on a major issue of policy, or not where individual rights were seriously affected, the minister must again acknowledge responsibility and ensure that corrective action was taken within the department. The minister was deemed not to be under such a constitutional duty where, otherwise than as above, the minister had no previous knowledge and disapproved of the action taken by the civil servant. This leads us to the second issue, that is, having taken responsibility for the actions of their civil servants, when are ministers under an obligation to resign?

It is notable that subsequent to the Crichel Down Affair there have been many instances of serious departmental failings that were not followed by ministerial resignations. Indeed, the only clear example of a resignation for a departmental failure since Crichel Down is that of Lord Carrington, who resigned as Foreign Secretary following allegations that the British forces were ill-prepared for the Argentinean attack at the start of the Falklands War. This has led some to suggest that the Crichel Down Affair represents the 'high water mark' for the classic doctrine of individual ministerial responsibility.

For example, in 1984, following a break-out of terrorists from the Maze Prison, James Prior, the then Northern Ireland Minister, refused to resign despite calls to do so. In parliamentary debate, the minister distinguished between his responsibilities for *policy* matters as opposed to *operational* matters. He asserted that he could not be held responsible for the failure of officials to carry out orders or procedures as instructed. Michael Howard adopted much the same reasoning in refusing to resign in 1994, following escapes from Whitemoor Prison. More recently, Stephen Byers resisted calls for his resignation after the failure of his department to make progress with plans for improvements to the transport infrastructure. He did eventually resign in 2002, though it is argued that this was more in response to pressure from the press than any obligation under the convention.

Other recent examples of ministerial resignations appear to result more from the failings or indiscretions of the ministers themselves than from the actions of their civil servants. For example, Edwina Currie resigned after creating a furore by stating that the majority of eggs in the UK were infected with salmonella. Nicholas Ridley similarly resigned after making inappropriate remarks about another Member State of the EU. Personal scandals would appear to provide the most common cause of resignation in recent times, such as in the cases of Cecil Parkinson, David Mellor, Jonathan Aitken, Peter Mandelson and Ron Davies.

In conclusion, it may be said that the size and complexity of modern government departments, as well as the frequently short tenure of ministerial office, make it impractical for a minister to assume responsibility for every decision taken. Furthermore, much has changed in the operation and structure of the civil service since Crichel Down. For example, much government departmental work has been 'hived-off' to semi-autonomous Next Step agencies responsible to their own chief executives.

The obligation to resign appears to play little part in the modern doctrine. Indeed, in *Ministerial Accountability* (1996), Sir Richard Scott, referring to the statement of Sir David Maxwell-Fyfe, argued that resignation is not 'at the heart of an effective system of Parliamentary accountability'. It was his view that the resignation of a minister served for nothing in bringing a clear account of events before Parliament. He believed that, rather than resignation, what lay at the centre of the doctrine of ministerial responsibility was 'An obligation of ministers to give, or to facilitate the giving, of information about the activities of their departments and about the actions and omissions of their civil servants'.

In the next chapter we consider further means by which the executive is held to account, in particular the parliamentary oversight provided by Select Committees and the judicial oversight provided by judicial public inquiries.

5 The legislature

The UK Parliament is composed of the Crown, the House of Lords and the House of Commons. At the end of this chapter we will also examine the devolution of power to the Northern Ireland Assembly, the Scottish Parliament and, to a lesser extent, the Welsh Assembly.

The House of Commons

The functions of the House of Commons

The functions of the House of Commons are:

- to represent the views and grievances of all sections of society;
- to scrutinise the executive;
- to legitimise Government actions.

State of the parties at January 2004

Party	Number of seats
Labour	408
Conservative	163
Liberal Democrat	54
Scottish National Party/Plaid Cymru	9 (SNP 5/PC 4)
Democratic Unionist	5
Sinn Fein	4 (have not taken their seats)
Social Democratic & Labour	3
Independent Unionist	3
Ulster Unionist	3
Independent/other	3
Speaker and 3 Deputies	4 (do not normally vote)
Total	**659**
Government majority	161

Composition and procedure in the House of Commons

There are 659 MPs divided across the two sides of the House, reflecting the adversarial nature of business in the House of Commons. Both sides of the House have front and backbenchers. The Speaker, acting with political impartiality, regulates the proceedings and controls debates in the House. The Speaker chooses who is allowed to speak in debate and will seek to respect the rights of minorities to participate. He or she also has powers of censure.

As we have already noted, under the constitution, Parliament ultimately exercises control over the Government in so far as it can withdraw its support. The very survival of the Government depends on this day-to-day support for its legislative programme. To counterbalance this parliamentary power, certain practices have developed over time to ensure that the Government of the day can count upon its legislative support.

The whips

With the growth in enfranchisement and universal adult suffrage came the corresponding growth in political parties. Originating as a loose association of like-minded individuals elected to office, these political parties soon developed an infrastructure and *whip system.* The purpose of the whip was (and still is) to maximise party effect by ensuring a disciplined collective vote on legislative matters.

It might be thought that it is not unreasonable for a Government comprising ministers drawn exclusively from members of one political party, predominantly within the House of Commons, to expect the support of colleagues committed to implementing the same election manifesto. Nevertheless, there has been criticism that the demands of party loyalty have done much to undermine the *individuality* of elected representatives, who, far from calling the executive to account for its legislative proposals, may be seen to act as mere lobby fodder for the party machine they serve.

Allocation of Parliament's time

On 75% of the days on which Parliament sits, Government business takes priority. The Opposition is allocated 20 days in each parliamentary session in which they can determine the business of the day. However, the main constitutional purpose of the Opposition is to probe and call the Government to account. Opportunities for others outside government to initiate debate are limited. Standing orders provide an opportunity to initiate an emergency debate, propose a Bill under the Ten Minute Rule or sponsor a Private Member's Bill. Furthermore, at the end of the day's business, members may initiate an adjournment debate on local or personal issues.

Clearly, parliamentary time is at a premium, and it is the task of the Leader of the House (responsible to the Prime Minister) to ensure that such time as is available is maximised to ensure the smooth passage of the Government's legislative programme for the parliamentary session. To this end, the Government has considerable procedural powers at its disposal, including the *guillotine* (allocation of time motion), under which the time made available for debate at one or more stages of a Bill can be restricted.

Legislative steps (through both Houses)

The planning of future Government legislation begins within cabinet and cabinet committees. Normally, prior to the introduction of a Bill on matters of public importance, there is a Green (that is, consultative) Paper and/or a White Paper (that is, a statement of policy). Formal stages of the legislative process begin with a *First Reading* (formal introduction of the proposal). This is followed by a *Second Reading* (where the principles of the Bill are considered). After its Second Reading, the Bill progresses to a *committee stage*. This usually takes place in a Standing Committee, but may be taken in Committee of the whole House or a special Standing Committee. The committee must consider each clause and Schedule of the Bill, agreeing or disagreeing to a motion that it 'stand part' of the Bill. The committee may also consider amendments to the Bill. Following this, the Committee reports to the House. Finally, the *Third Reading* and vote completes the Bill's passage through the House of Commons. The Bill then progresses to the House of Lords, where, although procedures vary, the stages are much the same as in the Commons. Once the Bill has received a Third Reading in the Lords, and agreement is reached between both Houses on any consequent amendments, it is presented for royal assent, which, by convention, should not be withheld.

Legislative steps by which a Government Bill becomes an Act of Parliament

Green Paper

White Paper

1st Reading

2nd Reading

Committee Report stage

3rd Reading

'Other place'

Royal Assent

Other legislation

Private Bills and Hybrid Bills Different parliamentary stages apply to Private Bills (which are promoted by individuals or bodies and generally relate to matters of private as opposed to public or general interest) and Hybrid Bills (which relate to matters of general interest, but in reality affect only the interests of certain individuals or organisations). Such Bills have limited success in becoming law but often serve to make a political point. The procedures involved and the statistics of their success are available on the House of Commons website (via www.parliament.uk).

Delegated legislation Statutory instruments (SIs) are a form of legislation that allows the provisions of an Act of Parliament subsequently to be brought into force, or altered without Parliament having to pass a new Act. They form the great bulk of the legislative provisions that become law in any session. They are also referred to as secondary or subordinate legislation. The scope of these powers varies greatly: on the one hand they may simply be technical, in so far as they provide the date on which different provisions of an Act come into force, or they may change the levels of fines or penalties for offences; on the other hand, they may provide much wider powers, for example, many parent Acts are drawn broadly, leaving secondary legislation to fill out the details. SIs are just as much a part of the law of the land as an Act of Parliament. However, it will be noted, in contrast to primary legislation, that the courts can question whether a minister, when issuing an SI, is acting within the powers actually given by the parent Act.

Parliamentary scrutiny The parent Act determines whether an instrument is subject to parliamentary procedure. Some SIs are not 'laid', and as such are not subject to any parliamentary procedure and simply become law on the date stated in them. Such instruments are, in general, not contentious. However, many SIs are subject to parliamentary control. The various procedures to be followed are laid down in the Statutory Instruments Act 1946.

To help with the parliamentary examination of SIs there is a Joint Committee of both Houses on Statutory Instruments (sometimes called the Scrutiny Committee). This Committee may, like other Select Committees, take oral or written evidence from the responsible Government department on any instrument it is considering. The Scrutiny Committee does not consider the merits of any SI. It is responsible for ensuring that a minister's powers are being carried out in accordance with the provisions of the enabling Act.

Scrutiny of the executive through parliamentary questions

Parliamentary question time in the House of Commons provides one of the principal means by which information can be obtained from ministers about their department, and necessarily underpins individual ministerial responsibility and accountability. Questions may be put to ministers for either oral or written answers.

Prime Minister's Questions (PMQs) occur once a week for 30 minutes. The questions posed by members should concern matters for which the Prime Minister carries responsibility and not matters that fall within an individual minister's responsibility. Generally, however, questions will concern overall Government policy in areas such as the economy, or foreign affairs or health. The strength of PMQs lies in the lack of notice given and the fact that the Prime Minister must be able respond to questions concerning any area of Government policy.

Scrutiny of the executive through Select Committees and public inquiries

The Select Committees of the House of Commons provide a more in-depth means to scrutinise the executive. Select Committees take various forms; some, for example, scrutinise proposed legislation, such as the European Legislation Committee or the Joint Committee (that is, of both Houses) on Human Rights. Departmental Select Committees are most obviously concerned with the issue of accountability. These were introduced in 1979 as a result of dissatisfaction with the previous means of monitoring departments. The committees have broad powers to examine the work of a department in any area they think appropriate. The extent to which Government can be called to account by these committees was exemplified by the Foreign Affairs Select Committee's examination of the decision to go to war in Iraq in 2003. The Committee rigorously questioned many of the leading participants, including the Foreign Secretary and the Prime Minister's then special adviser Alistair Campbell.

Nevertheless, some would argue that Select Committees are not effective enough in bringing Governments to account. For the most part Government departments do co-operate with Select Committees, but ministers cannot be compelled to attend before the committee or to answer specific questions. Limitations were particularly apparent following an investigation in 1992 by the Select Committee on Trade and Industry into the 'arms to Iraq' affair. The investigation concerned the supply of equipment to Iraq that allegedly could be used for military purposes. The Committee wished to establish information relating to the export licences, but was frustrated by a lack of co-operation from the Government. Separate judicial proceedings were brought against the directors of Matrix Churchill for obtaining these export licences without revealing the military nature of this equipment. At the trial it emerged that the Government was fully aware of these exports and had known all along of the intended use of the equipment. The scandal led to a *judicial inquiry* by Sir Richard Scott. Sir Richard's 1,800 page Report made a number of important findings, not least that Parliament had been 'deliberately' misled by Government ministers and that the Matrix Churchill trial 'ought never to have commenced'. There was also particular concern at the use of public interest immunity certificates during the trial to withhold information 'in the public interest', though the Report accepted that the Government had no intention of allowing innocent men to go to jail. In his assessment of the Scott Report, Professor Vernon Bogdanor noted: '... perhaps the deepest lesson of the Scott Inquiry is that Parliament is in danger of losing its capacity to bring ministers to account.'

The need for public inquiries?

The willingness of senior cabinet members, and even the Prime Minister himself, to appear before Select Committees in recent times perhaps suggests that some of the lessons of the Scott Inquiry have been learnt.

However, concerns regarding the effectiveness of Select Committees were once again voiced in the course of the Hutton Inquiry. The inquiry was established to investigate the suicide of Dr Kelly, a scientist and senior adviser, following the publication of a dossier on Iraqi weapons capabilities. The investigation concerned the issue of whether or not the relevant dossier had been 'sexed up' by Downing Street to further the case for war. A BBC journalist reported that this was Dr Kelly's view. The Government vehemently denied the allegation. The allegation had been investigated by both the Foreign Affairs Select Committee and the Intelligence and Security Committee. Some have argued that the subsequent judicial inquiry uncovered a great deal more of the background to the matter and was more revealing of the 'machinations' within Government than the Select Committees' reports, thereby criticising the Select Committees' effectiveness at getting to the bottom of matters in executive actions. However, this criticism perhaps overlooks the different mandate of the Hutton Inquiry – 'to conduct an investigation into the circumstances surrounding the death of Dr Kelly' – and the need for a wide-ranging public investigation where events have led to death. By contrast, the Intelligence and Security Committee's remit was limited to an examination of 'whether the available intelligence, which informed the decision to invade Iraq, was adequately and properly assessed and whether it was accurately reflected in government publications'.

The House of Lords

The functions of the House of Lords

The functions of the House of Lords are:

- as a forum for debate on matters of public interest;
- revision of Bills from the House of Commons;
- initiation of Bills;
- consideration of delegated legislation;
- scrutiny of the executive;
- Select Committee work;
- as the Supreme Court of Appeal.

Composition of House of Lords at January 2004 (by type)

Archbishops and bishops	24
Life Peers under the Appellate Jurisdiction Act 1876	27
Life Peers under the Life Peerages Act 1958 (109 women)	537
Peers under House of Lords Act 1999 (4 women)	92
TOTAL	**680**

Composition of House of Lords at January 2004 (by party strength)

Party	Life Peers	Hereditary	Bishops	Total
Conservative	160	49		209
Labour	181	4		185
Liberal Democrats	59	5		64
Cross bench	146	33		179
Archbishops and Bishops			24	24
Other	7			7
TOTAL	**553**	**91**	**24**	**668**[*]

* Excludes 12 peers on leave of absence.

Power and influence of the Lords

Parliament is *bicameral*, that is, it consists of two legislative chambers. The House of Lords is still referred to as the *Upper House*. At one time this accurately reflected its significance in relation to the other chamber, the House of Commons. But the continuing growth in democracy led to the elected *lower chamber* acquiring increasing significance until, at the beginning of the 20th century, it successfully challenged the Upper House for constitutional supremacy.

Prior to 1911, the House of Lords enjoyed equal powers with the Commons over legislation, except that, by convention, the Lords would not veto any financial measures. However, in 1909, a conflict arose when the Lords rejected a Finance Bill in breach of the convention. As a result of this conflict the Parliament Act 1911 was passed, which abolished the House of Lords' right to reject Money Bills and limited the time for which it could hold such Bills in review to one month. Furthermore, the Lords' rights to reject non-Money Bills was also abolished and replaced by a power to delay such Bills for a two-year period. Following further conflicts, the Parliament Act 1949 reduced the power of delay over non-Money Bills to one year. In reality the Parliament Acts are infrequently used, first, because the House of Commons accepts a great many of the amendments made in the Lords and, secondly, because the House of Lords is necessarily cautious about subverting the democratic authority of the Commons. Recent examples of the use of the Parliament Acts are the European Parliamentary Elections Act 1999 and the Sexual Offences (Amendment) Act 2000.

The importance of the House of Lords' function as a revising chamber should not be underestimated. Often the debate on legislation is far more in-depth and of a far better quality than in the House of Commons. The debate in the Commons on legislation is frequently marred by an adversarial approach and by party political point scoring. The debate in the Lords is usually more constructive than this, the quality of the speeches is high and overall the Lords have tended to be more liberal over social and moral rights. Some would argue that this results from the fact that the Lords do not currently have an electorate to please and that they are not subject to Government pressure to the same degree as their colleagues in the Commons. For example, the whips are less domineering and there is less use of the *guillotine* in debates. Thus, the members of the House of Lords are perhaps more readily able to view things in terms of the national interest than are their elected colleagues, who are obliged to take constituency and party interests into account. However, it has long been thought an anomaly that an unelected and unrepresentative chamber with its origins in patronage should hold power within the constitution.

Reform of the House of Lords

➥ Reform and proposals for reform:
- Parliament Act 1911
- Parliament Act 1949
- Leave of Absence Act 1958
- Life Peerages Act 1958
- Parliament (No 2) Bill 1969 (dropped after second reading)
- Peerage Act 1963
- House of Lords Act 1999

➥ Further proposals:
- *A House for the Future* – Royal Commission's Report (2000)
- *The House of Lords, Completing the Reform* – White Paper (2001)
- Joint Committee of House of Lords Reform (2002–)
  - First Report (December 2002)
  - Second Report (April 2003)
  - Government's response (July 2003)
- *Constitutional Reform: Next Steps for the House of Lords* – White Paper (2003)

The first phase of reform

Labour abandoned its abolitionist stance at the 1992 general election, and instead committed itself to the reform of the

House of Lords in its 1997 Manifesto. In 1998, there were 759 hereditary peers out of a total membership of 1,272. The first phase of reform, completed in Labour's first term, saw the removal of the majority of these hereditary peers under the House of Lords Act 1999. Ninety-two peers were allowed to remain for a transitionary period, though their right to sit will be axed at the next stage.

Concurrent with this legislation, proposals were made for an Appointments Commission; this began work in May 2000. It consists of representatives of the three main political parties and four independent figures. The Commission's present role is to make recommendations on non-party appointments, previously under the control of the Prime Minister. However, party appointments remain unchanged. It should also be remembered it is still the Prime Minister who passes on all recommendations to the Queen.

In April 2001 the Appointments Commission announced 15 nominations to the cross benches (dubbed 'the people's peers'). The announcement received criticism in the press on the basis that those nominated were the kind of establishment figures who might well have been nominated under the old system. However, it is doubtful whether the phrase 'the people's peers' adopted by the media correlates to the Commission's criteria for application. A date for a second round of appointments is yet to be set, but the Commission continues to accept nominations.

The second phase

The 2001 Labour Manifesto stated that the Government would complete the second phase of House of Lords reform by implementing the conclusions of the Royal Commission led by Lord Wakeham: *A House for the Future* (January 2000). A key recommendation of the Lord Wakeham's Report was the creation of a statutory Commission responsible for all appointments to a second chamber, not just cross benchers. This effectively would end party political appointments. Political parties could continue to submit names to the Commission, but there would be no guarantee that the Commission would decide to accept these nominations. Also of importance in the Wakeham recommendations were the proposals for a 'significant minority' of elected members.

Following on from this, the Government presented a White Paper to Parliament in November 2001 – *The House of Lords, Completing the Reform* – based on the following principles:

- The House of Lords should remain subject to the pre-eminence of the House of Commons in discharging its functions.
- No group in society should in future have privileged hereditary access to the House.
- The House of Lords' principal functions should continue to be to consider and revise legislation, to scrutinise the executive, and to debate and report on public issues.
- Membership should be separated from the peerage, which would continue as an honour.
- The House of Lords' political membership should be broadly representative of the main parties' relative voting strengths as reflected in the previous general election.
- Its membership should be largely nominated, including a significant minority of independent members as well as members elected to represent the nations and regions within the UK.
- There should be increased representation of women and those from ethnic minority backgrounds.
- There should be a statutory Appointments Commission to manage the balance and size of the House, to appoint the independent members, and to ensure the integrity of those nominated by political parties.

As regards composition, the White Paper proposed that the House of Lords would eventually consist of:

- 120 independent members appointed by the Appointments Commission;
- 120 directly elected members;
- 16 bishops;
- at least 12 Law Lords;
- a balance of not more than 332 nominated political members where the number available to each party is determined by the Appointments Commission.

The reaction of the press and many MPs to the White Paper was hostile. Despite the reform package being largely based on the recommendations of the Royal Commission, Lord Wakeham himself indicated that he would not back the proposals as they stood. This was due to the omission of certain key recommendations, including his recommendation for an independent Appointments Commission responsible for all appointments. By contrast, under the White Paper, party political appointments remained to over half the House. In addition, Lord Wakeham had recommended fixed terms for the elected element of as long as 15 years. The White Paper proposed just five-year terms. According to Lord Wakeham this was inappropriate for a revising chamber.

There followed continued division within Parliament and the Government itself, particularly over the issue of whether Lords should be elected or appointed and, if elected, to what proportion of the House. In a change of mind, the Prime Minister himself advocated a position contrary to the White Paper in supporting a fully appointed House of Lords.

With these continuing difficulties the White Paper's proposals on reform were abandoned. Instead, the Government passed the next stage on Lords reform to

Parliament. A Joint Committee of both Houses on reform was established, 'in the hope that we can forge the broadest possible parliamentary consensus for the way forward'.

However, the Joint Committee has met with little success in establishing consensus. Its First Report in December 2002 proposed a number of different compositions for the House of Lords, with varying numbers of elected members, ranging from fully appointed to fully elected. In February 2003 a vote was taken in both Houses on the various ratios, but other than the Lords themselves voting in favour of a fully appointed chamber, there was no consensus achieved on what composition was desirable. The basic objections to each alternative may be summarised as follows:

- A fully appointed House would amount to no reform at all as it would perpetuate the system of patronage that reform had sought to address.
- A fully elected House, on the other hand, would challenge the primacy of the House of Commons and undermine the current bicameral system of Parliament.
- A hybrid House of partly elected, partly appointed members would create a position where some members would have a greater mandate than others, and would be a fudged, constitutionally unstable compromise.

The result has been that reform has been stalled, or, as the Joint Committee put it in its Second Report in April 2003, 'Even if the engines have not actually fallen off the train, their thrust has been diminished'. However, the Joint Committee goes on to state that maintaining the status quo is unacceptable, and furthermore asserts that despite the lack of consensus on composition, there are many areas in which there is consensus, such as the value of maintaining the House's traditional legislative, revising and scrutinising functions. The Committee goes on to recommend that the debate should be widened beyond the narrow issue of numerical composition, and states its purpose to be:

> ... to wrestle with the objections to the past options we have put forward and endeavour to devise an electoral model which meets them – one which is democratic, which will lead to a membership which will make it both effective and legitimate, but which will ensure that the second chamber neither duplicates the composition of the Commons nor receives a mandate from the electorate which allows it to challenge the Commons' primacy.

The Committee proposes to look to models of *indirect election* to the second chamber and/or of *election by secondary mandate* (for an explanation of these models see the Second Report). In considering the way forward the Committee lists five qualities that it seeks to achieve in a reformed second chamber:

- legitimacy;
- representativeness;
- no domination by any one party;
- independence;
- expertise.

While consensus has not been achieved on the question of whether the Lords should be appointed or elected, the Government has nonetheless pushed ahead with other reforms. In June 2003, it produced White Papers on the abolition of the post of Lord Chancellor and the establishment of a Supreme Court and a Judicial Appointments Commission. In September 2003, the Government introduced a further White Paper, *Constitutional Reform: Next Steps for the House of Lords*. Its proposals are said to mark 'the next, but not the final, stage of Lords reform'. Proposals include the removal of the remaining hereditary peers and the transfer of many of the

Prime Minister's powers of appointment to a newly empowered Appointments Commission. The paper proposes that the Commission will determine the number and timing of appointments to be made to the House; select independent members entirely; and oversee party nominations, including vetting them on grounds of propriety. Clearly, this falls short of the promised second phase of reform, though the Government promises to consider further major reform in its next manifesto.

Devolution

Since coming to power in 1997, the Labour Government has brought about changes in devolved government in Scotland, Wales, Northern Ireland and London. However, Parliament at Westminster still retains its sovereignty and the Acts of Union have not been repealed:

- The Scotland Act 1998 was passed by Parliament pursuant to a referendum in September 1997. The resulting Scottish Parliament, which first met in 1999, has law-making power over the legal system, police and the penal system, economic development, industrial assistance, education and training, and also has tax-varying powers. It is elected every four years and elects a First Minister from among its number who then appoints an executive.
- The Government of Wales Act 1998 was passed following a poor vote of approval in a referendum of Welsh people in 1997. The Welsh Assembly has no tax-varying power and can make only secondary legislation. Its function is mainly to carry out the executive functions of the old Welsh Office. It is elected every four years and is headed by a First Minister elected from the Assembly who then appoints Assembly Secretaries.

➲ The Northern Ireland Act is primarily different because of the circumstances in which it was born, as it is intended to take into account the varying sections of the community that it represents. To this end there is an Assembly, North-South Ministerial Council, British-Irish Council and British-Irish Inter-Governmental Conference. The arrangements for devolved government were set out in the Good Friday Agreement, which had been agreed as a result of the peace process. The new institutions have not had an easy ride since power was devolved on 2 December 1999. Following another crisis in the peace process, the institutions of the devolved government in Northern Ireland were suspended, resulting in the re-imposition of direct rule. There had been three short suspensions in 2000 and 2001, but a fourth, indefinite period of suspension began in October 2002. Elections to the Assembly were held on 26 November 2003; however, the Assembly remains suspended.

➲ The Mayor of London has a wide range of specific powers and duties, and generally may do anything to promote the economic and social development of London. The Mayor is scrutinised by the London Assembly and together they make up the Greater London Assembly. Both are elected every four years.

Recent developments

A White Paper on regional assemblies in England appeared in 2002 but proposed only limited powers for elected regional assemblies. Proposed powers might include control of EU funds, housing funding allocations, tourism, heritage, museums, library functions, arts and sport funding. Following on from this, the Regional Assemblies (Preparations) Act 2003 was passed, but it deals only with referendums and electoral boundary reviews, and leaves the decision as to what powers a regional assembly would have, if established, to later legislation. Despite the Government's continuing commitment to regional government in England, the process is likely to be prolonged.

Following the successful 'bedding down' since devolution, a reshuffle in June 2003 remodelled the devolution arrangements at Westminster and Whitehall. The announcement saw the ending of full-time cabinet positions for the Scottish and Welsh Secretaries. The Scotland and Wales Offices have now been relocated within the newly created Department for Constitutional Affairs. It should be remembered that devolution does not alter the normal election of MPs to Westminster from constituencies in Scotland, Wales and Northern Ireland, though MPs may also hold seats in the regional parliament or assembly.

Electoral law

General election results 1979–2001

		1979	1983	1987	1992	1997	2001
Labour	Votes (%)	36.9	27.6	30.8	34.4	43.2	40.7
	Seats (%)	42.4	32.2	35.2	41.6	63.3	62.5
Conservative	Votes (%)	43.9	42.4	42.3	41.9	30.7	31.7
	Seats (%)	53.4	61.1	57.8	51.6	25.0	25.2
Liberal*	Votes (%)	13.8	25.4	22.6	17.8	16.8	18.3
	Seats (%)	1.7	3.5	3.4	3.1	7.0	7.9
Others	Votes (%)	5.3	4.6	4.3	5.9	9.3	9.3
	Seats (%)	2.5	3.2	3.6	3.7	4.8	4.4

* 1979: Liberal; 1983/1987: Liberal/SDP; 1992: Liberal Democrats.

First-past-the-post

The electoral system used in the UK for elections to the House of Commons is the *single member constituency with simple majority* system, also known as the *first-past-the-post* system (FPTP). The candidate who gets the largest number of votes is elected as Member of Parliament for that constituency, regardless of whether he or she has more than 50% support. The party with the most seats in Parliament, regardless of whether or not it has a majority across the country, normally becomes the next Government.

The advantages of this system are that it is a simple system for the voter to understand and, generally, it produces the clearest majorities. Clear majorities make for more stable government. However, on the other hand, 'landslide elections' are also more likely to occur, which can lead to an unaccountable executive. A greater criticism of FPTP is that the overall percentage of seats obtained in Parliament by a party is not proportionate to its overall percentage of votes in the country. The system works in such a way that if a party is consistently in second or third place across the country, it may have a substantial number of votes overall but obtain very few seats. For example, the Liberal parties in 1983 obtained a quarter of votes cast and yet obtained only 3.5% of seats in the House of Commons. By contrast, larger parties that win many constituency seats with less than 50 % of the vote gain a disproportionate number of seats. In 2001, Labour obtained 40.7% of the votes in the UK but 62.5% of the seats in Westminster. Targeting marginal constituencies in recent elections has enabled the Liberal Democrats to improve their ratio, but to many it remains an unsatisfactory return on votes cast.

Another argument against FPTP is that it renders a large proportion of votes ineffective. Only one MP is elected in each constituency, and therefore votes for unsuccessful candidates are simply wasted (in contrast to most Proportional Representation systems – see below). This may be a cause of voter apathy. In 'safe seat' constituencies, voters may feel that there is no point casting their vote at all, such as Conservative voters in Durham or Labour voters in Kensington.

Alternative systems

Most alternative systems are designed to make the number of seats won by a party more proportionate to the distribution of votes cast. Note that the generic term *Proportional Representation* (PR) is used for any system that introduces greater proportionality than FPTP.

Alternative electoral systems

Single-member systems	Multi-member systems	Mixed systems
➲ First-Past-the-Post (FPTP) ➲ Alternative Vote (AV) ➲ Supplementary Vote (SV)	➲ Single Transferable Vote (STV) ➲ Party List Systems	➲ Additional Member System (AMS) ➲ The Alternative Vote Plus (AV+)

Following the election in 1997, the Labour Government set up an Independent Commission, under the chairmanship of Lord Jenkins, to consider alternatives to FPTP. The Report summarised some of the main alternatives systems as follows:

➲ *The Alternative Vote (AV).* The Alternative Vote, which like FPTP is based upon single member constituencies, is a *majoritarian* system. Winning candidates must secure the support of over half the voters in a constituency. The vote is exercised by recording preferences against the candidates on the ballot paper. If no candidate receives more than half of the votes cast on the first count of first preference votes, the candidate who received the fewest first preference votes is eliminated and the voter's second preferences are distributed between the other candidates. This process continues until one candidate has achieved an overall majority. (A hybrid of this system is recommended for Westminster by the Jenkins Commission's Report – see below).

● *Supplementary Vote (SV)*. The Supplementary Vote system is similar in method and purpose to the Alternative Vote system, the key difference being that, under SV, voters are limited to indicating a first and second preference. Where candidates receive more than half of the first preference votes cast on the first count, they are deemed elected. If not, all but the top two candidates are eliminated and the second preferences on the ballot papers of the eliminated candidates are examined. The candidate with the greatest share of the resultant vote is elected. (This system is used to elect the Mayor of London.)

● *Single Transferable Vote (STV)*. The Single Transferable Vote system is essentially preferential voting (as in AV) in multi-member constituencies. Voters are able to rank as many candidates, both within parties and across different parties, as they wish in order of preference. Any of those candidates who reach a certain quota are deemed to have been elected. The surplus votes of candidates elected on the first count and the votes of those with fewest votes after subsequent counts are distributed on the basis of preferences to the remaining candidates until sufficient candidates reach the quota and are, as a result, elected. (This system is used in Northern Ireland, both for local elections and elections to the European Parliament (MEPs).)

⮕ *List Systems.* There are many variations of this system. However, the basic model is quite simple: rather than voting for a specific candidate, electors vote for a party in a multi-member constituency or region, or sometimes a whole country. All the votes are counted and each party receives seats in the constituency in the same proportion as the votes it won in that constituency or region. Each party has a list of candidates, ranked according to the party's preference, published on the ballot paper. Candidates will be elected in order of that ranking. (This system was used in mainland Britain for elections to the European Parliament in 1999; note that Northern Ireland used STV.)

⮕ *The Additional Member System (AMS).* This is a mixed system: basically, AMS is a combination of the FPTP system and a list system. The purpose is to retain the best features of FPTP while introducing proportionality between parties through party list voting. Under AMS, voters cast two distinct votes – the first for a constituency candidate and the second a party vote. The allocation of additional members then serves to correct the disproportionality that arises from the election of single constituency candidates. (This system is used to elect members to the Scottish Parliament, the Welsh Assembly and the London Assembly.)

Electoral reform for Westminster

In considering reform for Westminster elections, the *Jenkins Commission* assessed each of the systems against the background of four 'requirements'. These were:

- broad proportionality;
- the need for stable government;
- an extension of voter choice; and
- the maintenance of a link between MPs and geographical constituencies.

As the Commission pointed out, these four 'requirements' are not entirely compatible.

In its conclusions, the Jenkins Report (1998) recommended a mixed system, that is, an AV system with a 'top up' from a List System. The proposed system was termed *Alternative Vote Plus* (AV+). As with AMS, voters would have two votes – one for a constituency MP (elected on AV basis) and the other for a party of their choice. The Report suggested that 80–85% of MPs would be elected to their single seat constituency on an AV basis. In addition, to mitigate any disproportionality, a further 15–20% of MPs would be selected from a regional list according to the party vote.

The Government renewed its commitment to the reform of elections to Westminster in its 2001 election manifesto. It proposed to review the Jenkins proposals in the light of the experience of the new electoral systems already introduced for devolved government, the London Assembly and the European elections. It proposed that a referendum should be held before any changes are made at Westminster. Initial hopes that this would occur in the Government's second term have now evaporated. However, the positive reactions to the introduction of 'PR' type systems elsewhere in the UK have created the impetus for further reform (see further www.prcommission.org). A major concern with the current system remains voter apathy and poor turnouts.

Parliamentary privilege

Freedom of speech	Freedom to regulate composition	Freedom to regulate proceedings	Freedom from civil arrest	Power to punish for contempt

Both Houses of Parliament claim for their members privileges which, according to Erskine May's *Parliamentary Practice*, are necessary to each House, and without which they could not discharge their functions. Traditionally, Parliament claimed to be the sole and exclusive judge of its own privileges and of their extent (*Parliament Case* (1609)).

Privilege and the courts

The courts have recognised the existence of privileges and their necessity. In *Stockdale v Hansard* (1839), all the privileges required for the 'energetic discharge' of Parliament's functions were conceded by the court 'without a murmur or doubt'. In *Prebble v Television New Zealand Ltd* (1995), the Privy Council confirmed that the courts will not allow any challenge to be made to what is said or done within the walls of Parliament in relation to its legislative functions and the regulation of its established privileges. However, the courts have taken the view that it is for them to determine whether a matter before them truly falls within the realm of parliamentary privilege, especially if the rights of third parties are involved. In other words, it is not for Parliament alone to decide that privilege may be claimed in a particular case in order to exclude the jurisdiction of the courts. In *R v HM Treasury ex p Smedley* (1985), Donaldson MR stated:

> [It] behoves the courts to be ever sensitive to the paramount need to refrain from trespassing on the province of Parliament, or, so far as this can be avoided, even appearing to do so ... I would hope and expect that

Parliament would be similarly sensitive to the need to refrain from trespassing upon the province of the courts.

Privileges

Freedom of speech

Foremost of the privileges is freedom of speech in Parliamentary proceedings, provided by s 9 of the Bill of Rights 1689. The effect of this privilege was described by Cockburn LCJ in the case of *ex p Watson* (1869):

> It is clear that statements made by Members of either House of Parliament in their places in the House, though they might be untrue to their knowledge, could not be made the foundation of civil or criminal proceedings, however injurious they might be to the interest of a third party.

For a recent example see *R v A* (2002), where an individual failed in her attempt to seek redress in the courts against an MP who during parliamentary proceedings referred to her and her family as 'neighbours from hell'. The MP gave the woman's precise name and address, and consequently the family received hate mail and abuse and eventually had to be rehoused. The case also failed before the European Court of Human Rights (*A v UK* (2003)), where in finding that there was no breach of Article 6 or Article 8 of the ECHR, the Court commented that parliamentary immunity was a widely accepted principle that served the legitimate aim of ensuring freedom of speech in Parliament and was proportionate in the circumstances. The Court also commented that a victim of defamatory remarks made in Parliament was not entirely without redress as internal procedures of censure did exist, but redress was not a matter for the courts.

No immunity attaches to statements made outside Parliament. Press coverage, to the extent that it fairly and accurately reports parliamentary debates, is generally protected by a form of *qualified privilege* which is lost only if the publisher has acted 'maliciously'.

Parliament's right to control its own proceedings and composition

A central privilege is Parliament's exclusive right to control its own proceedings and composition. It is for Parliament alone to decide its procedures, and to decide whether to follow or depart from them. Even where Parliament administers its internal proceedings on the basis of an erroneous interpretation of statutory law, the courts have no power to interfere (*Bradlaugh v Gossett* (1884)). Neither will courts interfere with a decision by Parliament to exclude a duly elected member from the chamber (see *Allighan's Case* (1948) – a member was excluded for misconduct). Similarly, refusing an application for judicial review, the court indicated that it had no authority to challenge the decision of the Speaker to exclude members of Sinn Fein who refused to take the oath of allegiance to the Crown. The European Court of Human Rights also ruled the case inadmissible. However, the Government has recently allowed Sinn Fein members to use facilities at Westminster without swearing the oath of allegiance, though they remain barred from taking their seats.

Freedom from civil arrest

Members of both Houses enjoy freedom from civil arrest. There is no immunity from the provisions of criminal law. However, since there are now very few arrestable civil offences, the practical importance of this privilege is in providing an exemption from being summonsed as a witness.

Breach of privilege or contempt

Parliament also has the power to punish for contempt. Any act or omission that obstructs or impedes either House in the performance of its functions may be treated as contempt. Contempt may include acts that tend to diminish the respect due to Parliament and to lower its authority. It is for Parliament to decide how to punish a breach of privilege or contempt. Parliament has the power to commit individuals to prison, although the last time such a power was exercised was in 1880.

Parliamentary standards

Following on from the constitutional principle that Parliament remains free to regulate its own affairs without executive or judicial interference, it must also be responsible for regulating the standards of conduct of its members and for disciplining misconduct.

In 1994, following a number of highly publicised cases concerning government 'sleaze', the Committee on Standards in Public Life was established to deal with broad concerns about ethical standards. Following recommendations of the Committee's First Report, a *Parliamentary Commissioner for Standards* was appointed to investigate complaints about MPs. The Commissioner will only investigate complaints regarding:

- breaches of the Code of Conduct for Members of Parliament (see below);
- failure to register or declare relevant financial interests or benefits, as required by the rules laid down by the House;
- advocacy, where the member has a relevant financial interest;
- participation in delegations where the member has a relevant financial interest.

Following an investigation, the Commissioner will report to the Committee on whether the complaint is substantiated, and the

Committee will then decide what action to take, such as whether to suspend the MP.

The seven principles of public life

Selflessness Integrity Objectivity Accountability Openness Honesty Leadership

These principles come from the First Report of the Committee on Standards in Public Life:

⮥ *Selflessness*. Holders of public office should take decisions solely in terms of the public interest. They should not do so in order to gain financial or other material benefits for themselves, their family, or their friends.

⮥ *Integrity*. Holders of public office should not place themselves under any financial or other obligation to outside individuals or organisations that might seek to influence them in the performance of their official duties.

⮥ *Objectivity*. In carrying out public business, including making public appointments, awarding contracts, or recommending individuals for awards and benefits, holders of public office should make choices on merit.

⮥ *Accountability*. Holders of public office are accountable for their decisions and actions to the public and must submit themselves to whatever scrutiny is appropriate to their office.

⮥ *Openness*. Holders of public office should be as open as possible about all the decisions and actions that they take. They should give reasons for their decisions and restrict information only when the wider public interest clearly so demands.

⮥ *Honesty*. Holders of public office have a duty to declare any private interests relating to their public duties and to take steps to resolve any conflicts arising in a way that protects the public interest.

⮕ *Leadership.* Holders of public office should promote and support these principles by leadership and example.

Current concerns

The Committee on Standards in Public Life continues to report and make recommendations on many areas of parliamentary and government practice that raise 'current concerns'. For example, in its Ninth Report (2003) – *Defining the Boundaries within the Executive: ministers, special advisers and the permanent Civil Service* – the Committee addresses and makes recommendations on the topical issue of the appointment and status of special advisers.

6 The individual and the state

In Chapter 1 constitutional law was described as being concerned with the role and powers of state institutions and with the relationship between the citizen and the state. In this chapter we examine the relationship between the individual and the state, in particular the protections given by the common law and statute to the freedoms and liberties of the individual within the state. The entire landscape of this relationship has been crucially changed by the Human Rights Act 1998. We will examine the Act and its impact in some detail here, but for a full study guide the student is referred to the comprehensive *LawCard on Human Rights* (2003).

Historical basis for the protection of fundamental rights and liberties

Historically, the protection of an individual's fundamental rights and liberties in the UK, like the constitution itself, has lacked the certainty of a written declaration such as might be found in a comprehensive Bill of Rights. Apart from the protections provided by the four great statutes enacted to regulate the relations between the Crown and people – the Magna Carta of Edward I (1297), the Petition of Right (1627), the Bill of Rights (1689), and the Act of Settlement (1700) – containing general provisions to ensure the peaceful enjoyment of one's property, as well as freedom from illegal detention, duress, punishment or taxation, and apart from specific legislation conferring particular rights, the rights and liberties of the individual in the UK are not expressly defined in any distinct law or code. The changes to this position brought about by the enactment of the Human Rights Act 1998 are considered below, but it is important, first, to understand the underlying position.

Residual rights and liberties

> The starting point of our domestic law is that every citizen has a right to do what he likes, unless restrained by the common law or by statute. (*AG v Observer Ltd and others* (1990), *per* Sir John Donaldson MR)

Pursuant to the doctrine of parliamentary sovereignty, in English law there can be no set of legally entrenched, fundamental, positive rights existing beyond Parliament's countermand. Traditionally in English law, the liberties of the subject were merely implications drawn by the courts from two principles, namely:

- that you could do anything you wanted, provided there was no law against it; and
- that you could be assured that your individual rights would not be interfered with by a public authority unless there was express legal authority to do so under statute or the common law.

It is in this sense that the liberties of an individual are 'residual', as AV Dicey termed them, rather than fundamental and positive in their nature. However, Dicey's view was that this negative approach to defining liberties provided a more robust basis for their protection than would be afforded by a positive declaration of such rights in a constitutional document such as the *Déclaration des droits* in France. He pointed to the protection afforded to such rights and liberties in the UK, where the courts strictly and precisely defined the extent to which they might be interfered with under the existing statutory and common law, in contrast to the protection afforded by what was, in his view, the vague words of a positive declaration of such rights. In short, precisely defining the permissible limitations to such rights was more valuable and enforceable, in Dicey's view, than defining the rights themselves.

Dicey's contention was that constitutional documents such as the Bill of Rights in the US and the *Déclaration* in France were not automatic guarantees of the rights they contain, and indeed that they were little more than pious declarations in the absence of institutions with the willingness and integrity to apply them. As Dicey pointed out, many freedoms, such as the freedom of the press, were maintained with much more alacrity in the UK during the 19th century than, for example, in France, where the constitution of 1791 proclaims freedom of expression and the liberty of the press, and yet whose great writers were often published abroad due to restrictive press laws enacted in France after the revolution.

Dicey's thesis in modern Britain

Dicey's thesis on residual rights depended, however, upon the premise that laws would only ever impose narrow and tightly defined areas of liability, that Parliament would be an important check upon executive powers, and that the judiciary would construe laws strictly against any public authority seeking to interfere with an individual's liberties.

Dicey's thesis becomes less convincing in contemporary UK law. There has been much legislation that is not tightly or narrowly drawn in areas that may encroach upon civil liberties. Examples include the Criminal Justice and Public Order Act 1994 and the Anti-Terrorism, Crime and Security Act 2001. The growth of executive power has also led to criticisms that neither Parliament nor the judiciary are effective in ensuring that public powers are exercised in a manner protective of rights and liberties. Lord Bingham expressed the judiciary's powerlessness to protect fundamental rights in the absence of a 'higher' law:

> The elective dictatorship of the majority means that, by and large, the government of the day can get its way, even if its majority is small. If its programme or its practice involves some derogation from human rights Parliament cannot be relied on to correct this. Nor can judges. If the derogation springs from statute, they must faithfully apply the statute. If it is a result of administrative practice, there may well be no basis upon which they can interfere. There is no higher law, no frame of reference, to which they can properly appeal. ('The ECHR: time to incorporate' [1993] LQR)

Furthermore, Bills of Rights in many countries have proven to be far more than pious declarations and to be effective and important protections for the rights they contain. At the end of the 20th century, it was Britain, instead, that seemed to have lost an effective means of securing the rights and the liberties of its citizens. In an article in 1996, Ronald Dworkin lamented the loss of the culture of liberty in Britain:

> Great Britain was once a fortress for freedom. It claimed the great philosophers of liberty – Milton and Locke and Paine and Mill. Its legal tradition is irradiated with liberal ideas: that people accused of crime are presumed to be innocent, that no one owns another's conscience, that a man's home is his castle, that speech is the first liberty because it is central to all the rest. But now Britain offers much less formal legal protection to central freedoms than most democracies do, including most of Britain's neighbours in Europe. These democracies have written constitutions that guarantee individual freedom, and their judges are charged with ensuring that other public officials, including legislators, respect those rights. (*Does Britain Need a Bill of Rights?*)

Significance of the European Convention on Human Rights

It was stated above that the doctrine of parliamentary sovereignty prevents the entrenchment of fundamental rights in English law, but it is still the fact that the UK is party in international law to instruments such as the Universal Declaration on Human Rights (UDHR) and the European Convention on Human Rights (ECHR). The latter is of particular significance in that it has an enforcement mechanism – a citizen can go to the European Court of Human Rights (ECtHR) in Strasbourg to enforce his or her rights under the Convention against the UK.

However, prior to incorporation of the ECHR into domestic law, there was no means for an individual to enforce such rights in the national courts. This is due to the 'dualist' approach to international law inherent in English law. Under this approach, pursuant to the doctrine of parliamentary sovereignty, domestic and international law are entirely distinct and separate, governing different areas and relationships, and different in substance. Furthermore, international law is 'inferior' in so far as it can only ever become part of domestic law by being incorporated by further domestic legislation. In the UK the legal system is entirely dualist and there are no provisions for international law to be 'self-executing'. So, for example, prior to incorporation of the ECHR, in *Malone v Metropolitan Police Commissioner (No 2)* (1979), Vice-Chancellor Megarry stated that 'the Convention is not law here'. (For further details of the dualist approach to international law, see Chapter 3.)

An aid to interpretation

While the courts had no jurisdiction to enforce the rights under the Convention, nonetheless, the ECHR was still an important aid to the interpretation of 'ambiguous' domestic legislation. In *R v Secretary of State for the Home Department ex p Brind* (1991), Lord Bridge enunciated the basic law of interpretation:

> ... But it is already well settled that, in construing any provision in domestic legislation which is ambiguous in the sense that it is capable of a meaning which either conforms to or conflicts with the Convention, the courts will presume that Parliament intended to legislate in conformity with the Convention, not in conflict with it.

In the period leading up to the Human Rights Act 1998, the courts relied increasingly on the Convention in construing legislation in favour of protecting fundamental rights: see, for example, the decision of the Court of Appeal in *Derbyshire County Council v Times Newspapers Ltd* (1993). Nevertheless, the limitation remained: the courts had no jurisdiction to enforce Convention rights. If the meaning of a statute was clear and unambiguous, the court had to give effect to it, whether or not it derogated from fundamental rights: see *R v Inland Revenue Commissioners ex p Rossminster Ltd* (1980).

For an overview of the structure of the European Convention on Human Rights, see *LawCard on Human Rights* (2003).

Human Rights Act 1998: positive entitlements

The Human Rights Act (HRA) 1998 is the culmination of a long campaign for the incorporation into domestic law of the ECHR. The Act is generally regarded as providing an ingenious solution to the problem of protecting fundamental rights while maintaining parliamentary sovereignty. However, the radical changes in UK law produced by the Act should not be underestimated.

According to Lord Irvine, the origins of the Act are to be found in the Government's perception that:

> ... the traditional freedom of the individual under an unwritten constitution, to do himself that which is not prohibited by law, gives inadequate protection from misuse of power by the State, nor any protection from acts or omissions by public bodies which harm individuals in a way that is incompatible with fundamental rights. That is why we were determined to introduce a rights based system under which people's rights were asserted as positive entitlements expressed in clear and principled terms. (*Government's Programme of Constitutional Reform* (1998), lecture by Lord Irvine)

New protections

The 1998 Act introduced new protections for fundamental rights:

- a strong new rule of construction; and
- declarations of incompatibility.

New rule of construction (s 3)

In line with the doctrine of parliamentary sovereignty, the Act does not empower the courts to strike down incompatible primary legislation. The approach is 'interpretative' only. Section 3 requires that:

> So far as it is possible to do so, primary legislation and subordinate legislation must be read and given effect in a way which is compatible with the Convention rights.

As noted above, previously the court was only enabled to take the Convention into account in resolving an ambiguity in a legislative provision. According to the Lord Irvine, this new rule of construction

> goes far beyond the [previous] rule. It will not be necessary to find an ambiguity. On the contrary the courts will be required to interpret legislation so as to uphold the Convention rights unless the legislation itself is so clearly incompatible with the Convention that is impossible to do so.

Further, he approved the use of the same interpretative techniques as used to ensure that domestic legislation complies with EC law:

> ... even when this requires straining the meaning of words or reading in words which are not there. (*Tom Sargant Memorial Lecture* (1998))

On this basis we can see that the Act provides a powerful new basis for the courts to protect fundamental rights in the cases before them. For example, in *R v A* (2001), the House of Lords adopted an extremely creative interpretative approach by reading implied words into a legislative provision. The case concerned the interpretation of s 41(3)(c) of the Youth Justice and Criminal Evidence Act 1999, which in rape cases provides that, where consent is in issue, evidence of any sexual behaviour of the complainant will not be admissible. The House of Lords read into s 41(3)(c) an implied qualification that evidence that is necessary to ensure a fair trial under Article 6 ECHR should not be rendered inadmissible by the section, and therefore such evidence could be adduced in relation to the issue of consent. To use Lord Steyn's words, this was an interpretation 'which linguistically will appear strained'. It was clearly contrary to the 'unambiguous' intention of the legislature.

Declarations of incompatibility

Primary legislation   As has already been stated, the 1998 Act provides no basis for the courts to strike down primary legislation. However, s 4(4) provides that:

> If the court is satisfied–
> (a)   that the provision is incompatible with a Convention right, and
> (b)   that (disregarding any possibility of revocation) the primary legislation concerned prevents removal of the incompatibility,
> it may make a declaration of that incompatibility.

Lord Irvine explained the impact of s 3 and s 4 taken as a package:

> The [Act] sets out a scheme for giving effect to the Convention rights which maximises the protection to individuals while retaining the fundamental principle of parliamentary sovereignty. Section 3 is the central part of the scheme. Section 3(1) requires legislation to be read and given effect to so far as is possible to do so in a way that is compatible with Convention rights. Section 3(2) provides that where it is not possible to do so … that does not affect its validity, continuing operation or enforcement. This ensures the courts are not empowered to strike down Acts of Parliament which they find to be incompatible with Convention rights. Instead s 4 of the Act … introduces a new mechanism through which the courts can signal to the Government that a provision of legislation is, in their view, incompatible. It is then for government and Parliament to consider what action should be taken. (HL, Report stage of the Bill)

The expected approach to the making of declarations was outlined by the then Home Secretary in the House of Commons:

> We expect that, in almost all cases, the court will be able to interpret legislation compatibly with the Convention. However, we need to provide for the rare cases where that cannot be done ...

Where a declaration of incompatibility is made under s 4, the Home Secretary continued:

> ... it is likely that the Government and Parliament would wish to respond to such a situation and would do so rapidly. (HC, 3 June 1998)

Subordinate legislation As previously, the court has jurisdiction to strike down subordinate legislation on normal *ultra vires* grounds (see Chapter 7), though the Act introduces a new basis to do so if the subordinate legislation is incompatible with a Convention right. However, it should be noted that s 3(2)(c) creates a distinction between incompatible subordinate legislation where the parent Act prevents removal of the incompatibility, and incompatible subordinate legislation where that is not the case. In the case of the former, the subordinate legislation remains valid, since to hold otherwise would be to disregard a provision of primary legislation, though a declaration of incompatibility may be made under s 4(4) (see above).

Other important provisions of the HRA 1998

- Power to take remedial action (s 10).
- Statements of compatibility on the face of new legislation (s 19).
- Functional definition of public authorities (s 6).
- Inclusion of courts and tribunals as 'public authorities' (s 6(3)).
- Special provisions in relation to Article 10 ECHR (freedom of expression) and Article 9 ECHR (freedom of thought, conscience and religion) (ss 12 and 13).

Remedial action (s 10)

Section 10 is an important innovation of the HRA 1998 and provides fast-track procedures for amending legislation either (i) where a declaration of incompatibility has been made, or (ii) in response to a finding of the ECtHR.

In normal circumstances any amendment to legislation must be made by Parliament, but in some circumstances the Government will want to bring legislation into line with human rights requirements more quickly than the normal parliamentary process allows. In such case a remedial order to amend legislation (primary or secondary) may be made by a minister. It may be made only after the appeal process has been exhausted, and there must be 'compelling reasons' to do so.

Statements of compatibility (s 19)

Section 19 is one of the novel features of the Act and is potentially very important. Ministers are required to make a statement on the face of all new Bills as to whether the provisions of the new legislation are compatible with the Convention. The requirement should have a significant impact on the scrutiny of draft legislation within government. Where such a statement cannot be made, parliamentary scrutiny of the Bill is likely to be intense.

Limits of claims under the Act

The limitations of the Act should not be forgotten:

- Limited to public authorities – no 'direct' horizontal effect (s 6).
- Claimant must be a 'victim' (s 7).
- Declarations may be made only by higher courts.
- Declarations are not a remedy for a claimant.

➲ No obligation to amend legislation in response to a declaration.

➲ Derogations permissible.

Victims and public authorities

Section 7 provides that a claim may be brought only by a 'victim', and this therefore precludes claims by pressure groups (compare this with the position in ordinary judicial review proceedings considered in Chapter 7). Furthermore, Convention rights can only be enforced against 'public authorities', as defined in s 6(3), and therefore such rights cannot be directly relied upon in proceedings between private parties. This led to some anomalous results, such as in *R (Heather) v Leonard Cheshire Foundation* (2002). The Foundation, a private charity, provides accommodation for the disabled: some of their homes are funded by the local authority; some are not. The court held that only those residents of homes funded by the local authority could rely on their Convention rights; the other residents could not.

Indirect horizontal effect

Much has been made of the inclusion of courts and tribunals under s 6(3)(a). This inclusion requires them to act compatibly with Convention rights, and therefore, it is argued, this creates what has been called an 'indirect' horizontal effect. In other words, although the parties in private proceedings will not be able to rely on Convention rights directly, the courts have a duty to apply the law compatibly with Convention rights in those proceedings. That duty includes both interpreting legislation and developing the common law in line with the Convention, in effect giving the Act horizontal application.

That legislation will be interpreted compatibly with Convention rights in private proceedings is uncontroversial, but the extent to which the common law will be developed in such proceedings to protect Convention rights is less clear. In considering the impact of the HRA 1998 in *Douglas v Hello!* (2001), Sedley LJ posed the question: does s 6(3)(a) simply require the courts' procedures to be Convention-compliant, or does it require the law applied by the court to give effect to Convention principles, even where proceedings are between private parties? He was unwilling to answer the question in respect of all Convention rights, but in relation to Article 8 rights Sedley LJ's view was that the impetus of the HRA was such that the existing common law doctrine of breach of confidence could be developed to protect Article 8 rights.

Declarations of incompatibility

Only the higher courts have the power to make a declaration under s 4; yet where is the incentive for the 'victim' to take the matter to the higher courts where that court remains obliged to enforce incompatible primary legislation? It is important to underline that a declaration does not provide a remedy for the 'instant' claimant. For example, in *R (H) v Mental Health Review Tribunal* (2001), under provisions of the Mental Health Act 1983, the Review Tribunal could release a mental health patient from detention only if it satisfied itself that the patient was *not* suffering from mental disorder, rather than positively being satisfied that he was so suffering. In effect this placed the onus of proof on the restricted person, and as such could not be construed by the court as compatible with Article 5 of the Convention, and a 'declaration of incompatibility' was made. The fact that the tribunal was obliged to act incompatibly by primary legislation meant that its actions remained lawful, and therefore there was no successful cause of action for the applicant. However, this case generated the first remedial order under s 10 of the HRA

1998, and subsequent review of H's detention placed the burden of proof on the tribunal.

Furthermore, it is important to remember that where a declaration of incompatibility is made, there is no obligation on the minister or Parliament to amend the relevant legislation. For example, the penalty regime imposed on lorry drivers for carrying illegal entrants under the Immigration and Asylum Act 1999 was held to be incompatible with the ECHR in *International Transport Roth GmbH v Secretary of State for the Home Department* (2002). However, there have been no moves by the Government to remedy or amend the legislation.

Derogation

Article 15 ECHR provides that:

> In time of war or other public emergency threatening the life of the nation any High Contracting Party may take measures derogating from its obligations under this Convention to the extent strictly required by the exigencies of the situation, provided that such measures are not inconsistent with its other obligations under international law.

Under this Article, the Government derogated from Article 5 (right to liberty) in respect of provisions in the Anti-terrorism, Crime and Security Act 2001 for the indefinite detention, without charge, of suspected international terrorists. The fact that Convention rights can be derogated from in this manner has caused much concern amongst civil libertarians.

Limitations of the ECHR itself

Brief mention should be made of the inherent limitations to the protections afforded by the ECHR:

- the age of the Convention;
- its wide-ranging exceptions; and
- the missing rights.

The age of the Convention and its wide-ranging exceptions

The ECHR is over 50 years old, and it is argued that at times the meaning of the text is stretched to a point of distortion in order to protect particular rights. For example, Article 8 has been held to provide adult gay men with protection from prosecution for consensual sexual intercourse (*Dudgeon v UK* (1981)), an interpretation that would not have occurred to those who drafted the Convention. There are also a number of anachronisms in the ECHR, including the right under Article 5(1)(e) to imprison vagrants, alcoholics and those likely to spread infectious diseases. There is also the criticism that the many of the Convention rights, such as the right to freedom of expression or family life, are qualified by a number of exceptions primarily tailored to the interests of state institutions.

Missing rights

The absence of certain rights from the Convention has also been highlighted. For example:

- the ECHR is limited to civil and political rights as opposed to social and economic rights;
- there is no 'right to know';
- there is a limited right to trial for immigrants and asylum seekers;
- there is only a weak right to privacy;
- there are no specific rights for children;
- the anti-discrimination Article is weak.

The absence of a 'right to know' was much debated. Public scrutiny both of policy formulation and of the basis of decision taking is central to securing civil liberties and ensuring that a 'rights based culture' develops within Government itself. Partially in response to these arguments, and in order to supplement the Human Rights Act, the Labour Government did introduce the Freedom of Information Act (FOIA) 2000, though it is not in force until 2005. This is a positive development from the previous position where there was no legal basis to obtain information, but the FOIA is severely limited, particularly regarding access to Government information, which is heavily guarded by class exemptions and a ministerial veto. See 'A little bit of singing and a little bit of dancing: the FOIA and open government', *Student Law Review*, 2002, by Graham Arnold.

Judicial review

In Chapter 7 we examine in further detail the impact of the HRA on judicial review, and in particular its impact upon the traditional grounds for review.

Summary: raising Convention rights under the HRA 1998

The chart opposite summarises the operation of the Act.

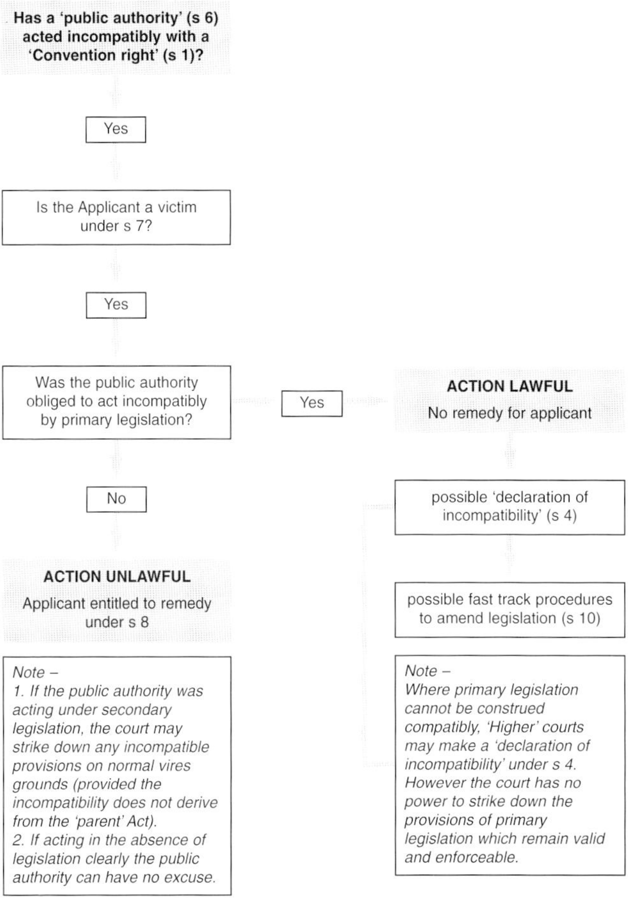

Has a 'public authority' (s 6) acted incompatibly with a 'Convention right' (s 1)?

Yes

Is the Applicant a victim under s 7?

Yes

Was the public authority obliged to act incompatibly by primary legislation?

Yes

ACTION LAWFUL

No remedy for applicant

possible 'declaration of incompatibility' (s 4)

possible fast track procedures to amend legislation (s 10)

No

ACTION UNLAWFUL

Applicant entitled to remedy under s 8

Note –
1. If the public authority was acting under secondary legislation, the court may strike down any incompatible provisions on normal vires grounds (provided the incompatibility does not derive from the 'parent' Act).
2. If acting in the absence of legislation clearly the public authority can have no excuse.

Note –
Where primary legislation cannot be construed compatibly, 'Higher' courts may make a 'declaration of incompatibility' under s 4. However the court has no power to strike down the provisions of primary legislation which remain valid and enforceable.

Particular areas of restriction

Having examined the general landscape for the protection of rights and liberties in the UK, you should also consider specific restrictions on rights and freedoms imposed by statute and the common law. Such restrictions are generally imposed in the 'public interest'. We briefly examine examples in the following contexts:

- Freedom of expression.
- Freedom of association and assembly.
- Police powers.
- National security and official secrecy.

Freedom of expression

The right to freedom of expression, particularly the freedom to criticise public bodies, is regarded by the courts as fundamental (*Derbyshire County Council v Times Newspapers Ltd* (1993)). However, the right, as laid down in Article 10 ECHR, is subject to certain restrictions on grounds of:

- national security;
- censorship;
- contempt of court;
- defamation;
- public order; and
- privacy.

Free speech is positively encouraged in a number of ways, such as in the absolute privilege of Members of Parliament and in the qualified privilege and defences to defamation available to newspapers, radio and television broadcasts and other media. Article 10 ECHR, as now incorporated by the HRA 1998, sets out the right in positive terms. Nevertheless, the right is limited by such restrictions as are necessary in a democratic society, in the interests of national security, territorial integrity or public safety, for the prevention of disorder or crime, for the protection of health or morals, for the protection of the reputation or rights of others, for preventing the disclosure of information received in confidence, or for maintaining the authority and impartiality of the judiciary. (Article 10(2) ECHR)

Similarly, under existing statute and common law, free speech is restricted by competing public interests. Examples include:

- *National security.* The criminal law provides restrictions, for example: offences under the Official Secrets Acts 1911 and 1989; treason; sedition; incitement to mutiny or disaffection. The state can also restrict free speech under the doctrine of confidentiality: see *AG v Jonathan Cape Ltd, AG v Times Newspapers Ltd* (1976) regarding the publication of diaries of a cabinet minister.
- *Censorship.* There are a number of restrictions on obscene and corrupting or otherwise offensive material. For example, see the Children and Young Persons (Harmful Publications) Act 1955; Obscene Publications Act 1959; Theatres Act 1968; Indecent Displays (Control) Act 1981; Public Order Act 1986, s 20.
- *Defamation law* also provides restrictions on freedom of speech by imposing criminal and civil liability for slander or libel.
- *Interests of the fair administration of justice.* See the Contempt of Court Act 1981 and other common law restrictions on interfering with the course of justice. In *R v Sherwood ex p Telegraph Group* (2001), the Court of Appeal indicated that restrictions on media coverage of court proceedings were a matter of balancing Article 10 rights and Article 6 rights (right to a fair trial).

➲ *Public order restrictions.* Provisions under the Public Order Act 1986 restrict the use of offensive or threatening words or material inciting racial hatred.

There has been much debate about the impact of the HRA 1998 on the freedom of the press and the clash with rights to privacy. Lobbying from press organisations resulted in s 12 being added to the Act. Section 12 applies where the court is considering whether or not to grant an injunction against publication – for example, restricting a newspaper from publishing photographs that may intrude upon an individual's privacy. In such circumstances, s 12(4) requires the court to have 'particular regard' to Article 10 rights, taking into account whether or not the material is already in the public domain, whether there are any public interest reasons for publishing, and having regard to any privacy code such as the Press Complaints Commission's code which outlines standards of behaviour to be expected of the press. The intention of the section was to bolster the freedom of the press against claims of privacy, however it has not deterred the courts from expanding the common law to protect Article 8 rights where press intrusions are excessive. See *Douglas v Hello!* (2002).

Freedom of association and assembly

➲ Breach of the peace.
➲ Public order.
➲ Proscribed organisations.

Article 11 ECHR provides that:

> Everyone has the right to freedom of peaceful assembly and to freedom of association with others, including the right to form and to join trade unions ...

However, once again, the right is qualified by such public interest restrictions as are 'necessary in a democratic society'.

In addition, these freedoms are subject to regulation by both common law and statute. The common law removes certain rights from a person who commits or who threatens to commit a breach of the peace: see *R v Howell* (1982). There also are several statutory offences that limit the right to free assembly. The Public Order Act 1986 provides for offences of riot, violent disorder, affray, causing fear of or provoking violence, or causing harassment, alarm or distress. Under s 11 of the Act, the police have powers to regulate demonstrations and may apply to have them prohibited. Also, s 1 of the Public Order Act 1936 makes it an offence to wear a uniform in any public place, or at any public meeting, signifying association with any political object. Furthermore, special restrictions apply to associating with quasi-military organisations and other proscribed organisations deemed to be detrimental to the interests of the state (as listed in Sched 2 to the Terrorism Act 2000).

Police powers

- Stop and search.
- Arrest.
- Seizure of property.
- Detention.

A balance has to be struck between an individual's civil liberties and the requirements of the administration of the criminal justice system, including the provision of police powers. The Police and Criminal Evidence Act (PACE) 1984 was introduced with the aim of putting police powers on a clear statutory footing and at the same time providing greater procedural safeguards for suspects:

- ss 24 and 25 provide for the powers of arrest;
- s 17 provides power to enter a home to effect an arrest;

↷ s 18 provides that, immediately after arrest, if there are reasonable grounds, an officer may search premises for evidence;

↷ s 19 provides power to seize items in relation to an offence;

↷ the Act also sets out detailed provisions on the purpose and time limits of detention of a suspect at a police station.

A number of other statutes also provide legal powers of 'stop and search', such as the Misuse of Drugs Act 1971.

Rules are made under PACE 1984 that constrain the police in the operation of these formidable powers. In addition, under the Act, a number of Codes of Practice have been issued. The Codes do not have the force of law but represent an important means of regulating the use of police powers:

↷ Code A: stop and search procedures.
↷ Code B: searching of premises.
↷ Code C: interviewing and detention.
↷ Code D: identification procedures.
↷ Code E: tape recording of interviews.

National security and official secrecy

↷ Official secrecy.
↷ Interception of communications.
↷ Emergency powers.
↷ Terrorism.

Security of the state

The security of the state is of the greatest importance, both to the individual and to the state. On the other hand, the rights and freedoms of individuals may be curtailed in the pursuit of such security. The state may justify interference with civil liberties on national security grounds in a wide range of areas, for example in the removal of the right to union membership at GCHQ in *CCSU v Minister of State for Civil Service* (1985), or in the deportation of an individual in *R v Home Secretary ex p Cheblak* (1991), or in the tapping of private telephone calls in *R v Secretary of State for the Home Department ex p Ruddock* (1987).

Official secrecy

Areas of official secrecy provide particular curtailments on the freedoms of individuals. Official secrets are protected by a number of statutes. The Official Secrets Acts (1911–1989), besides providing severe penalties for activities connected to spying and sabotage, also place severe restrictions on an individual's freedom of expression. A person who is or has been a member of the security or intelligence services is guilty of an offence if without lawful authority he discloses any information relating to security or intelligence obtained in the course of his service. A person prosecuted under the 1989 Act cannot rely on the defence of making a disclosure in the public or national interest: see *R v Shayler* (2002). In relation to official secrets, the restriction on press publication is governed by the voluntary 'DA' (Defence Advisory) notice system.

Interception of communications

Rights and freedoms are also subject to restrictions authorised under the Regulation of Investigatory Powers Act 2000. The Act provides powers to the Secretary of State to authorise covert surveillance, including the interception of private communications, in 'the interests of national security' and for 'the purpose of preventing or detecting serious crime'.

Emergency powers

Additional powers are available to the state in times of emergency, such as when serious civil unrest occurs in peacetime or in times of war. Such powers may lawfully encroach upon rights and freedoms. In peacetime emergencies, the Emergency Powers Acts 1920 and 1964 confer on the Government such powers and duties as may be deemed 'necessary for the preservation of the peace'. In wartime, the Defence of the Realm Acts 1914–15 conferred wide powers on the Government to make regulations in the interests of defence and public safety. It should be noted that there are also specific 'emergency' provisions for Northern Ireland contained in Part VII of the Terrorism Act 2000, providing additional powers to the authorities there.

Terrorism

There has been a considerable amount of legislation designed to counter terrorism both in Northern Ireland and on the mainland, including the Terrorism Act 2000 and the Anti-terrorism, Crime and Security Act 2001. The legislation provides for a number of terrorist offences, and also prohibits membership, support or association with regard to proscribed organisations. It is also an offence for a person to collect, make a record of, publish, communicate or attempt to elicit information which is of a kind likely to be useful to a person committing or preparing an act of terrorism, There are extended police powers to deal with suspected terrorists, including additional powers of arrest, search, seizure of property, and powers to demand the removal of facial coverings or face paint for the purposes of identification, as well as powers to cordon off and close highways. Following on from the terrorist attack in New York on 11 September 2001, the 2001 Act provides additional powers to strengthen security in aviation and nuclear industries. Of particular controversy with regard to civil liberties issues are the provisions in the Act for the extended detention of suspected international terrorists under Part 4, ss 21–32. Under the provisions, a foreign individual certified by the Secretary of State to be a suspected international terrorist may be detained indefinitely without charge in circumstances where either a legal impediment derived from an international obligation, or a practical consideration prevents deportation. These provisions required the Government to derogate from Article 5(1) ECHR. Detention under the provisions is regularly review by the Special Immigration Appeals Commission (SIAC), but detention is excluded from judicial review.

7 Judicial review

Introduction

Judicial review is the process by which the courts exercise a supervisory role over the acts and omissions of public bodies in the field of public law.

The process, grounds and remedies of judicial review

Preliminary Issues	Grounds	Remedies
⮑ Procedure ⮑ Permission ⮑ Delay ⮑ Standing ⮑ Public law body? ⮑ Public law issue?	⮑ Illegality ⮑ HRA illegality ⮑ Irrationality ⮑ Procedural impropriety	⮑ Quashing order ⮑ Prohibitory order ⮑ Mandatory order ⮑ Damages ⮑ Injunction ⮑ Declaration

Meaning of judicial review

Section 31 of the Supreme Court Act (SCA) 1981 and Part 54 of the Civil Procedure Rules (CPR) 1998 provide the rules applicable to judicial review. Applications for judicial review are heard by the Administrative Court, a subdivision of the Queen's Bench Division of the High Court, staffed by judges experienced in this type of claim. The powers of review are only available against public bodies in relation to their public functions and a claim can only be brought by a person with 'sufficient interest' in the matter (s 31(3) of the SCA 1981).

CPR r 54.1(2)(a) provides:

(a) 'claim for judicial review' means a claim to review the lawfulness of–
(i) an enactment; or

(ii) a decision, action or failure to act in relation to the exercise of a public function.

Constitutional limits of judicial review

Later in this chapter we will consider the constitutional limits to the judicial review of enactments, particularly in respect of primary legislation. However, at this stage, it should be noted that, in principle, judicial review is limited to a review of the lawfulness or *legality* of a decision by a public body – in general the courts do not review the *merits* of a decision, or consider whether a more appropriate decision should have been taken. (The exception is the limited merits-based review allowed under the principles of *Wednesbury unreasonableness* and proportionality – see below.) This distinction is a fundamental principle of public law in the UK. The traditional view is that the courts will ensure that public bodies act legally within their powers – or *intra vires* – and that they observe the rules of natural justice (see below), but within those boundaries the public body should not have the merits of its decisions challenged by the courts. This deference to executive and administrative decision-making is in line with the constitutional doctrines of parliamentary sovereignty and the separation of powers. In principle, public bodies derive their authority from Parliament and ultimately from the electorate, and it is not for unelected judges to step into their shoes (*per* Laws LJ in *R v Secretary of State ex p Mahmood* (2001)). The judges have frequently stressed the necessity of this limitation upon the powers of review. The purpose of judicial review was summarised by Lord Hailsham in *Chief Constable of North Wales Police v Evans* (1982):

> In every case ... the purpose of [judicial review] is to ensure that the individual is given fair treatment by the authority to which he has been subjected and that it is no part of that purpose to substitute the opinion of the judiciary or of

individual judges for that of the authority constituted by law to decide the matters in question. The function of the court is to see the lawful authority is not abused by unfair treatment and not to attempt itself the task entrusted to that authority by the law.

Distinction between review and appeal

From the above, we can establish that there is a clear distinction between review and appeal. In an appeal, the court will have the power to decide whether a decision was right or wrong and, if wrong, it is generally permitted to substitute its own decision for the erroneous one. By contrast, in judicial review the court is limited to a supervisory role, in so far as it is concerned not with the decision itself but with the decision-making process. If the court finds the latter to be flawed then it may quash the decision, but it will then be for the decision maker to reconsider the decision, and there is no guarantee that it will not reach the same decision again, albeit with a corrected decision-making process.

An application for judicial review

There are four principal questions to be answered:

- Which public bodies or persons are amenable to judicial review?
- Is the decision, act or omission challenged amenable to judicial review?
- On what grounds does judicial review lie?
- Who can apply?

Public bodies or persons amenable to judicial review

A claim for judicial review may be brought against inferior courts, tribunals, or any body or person performing public duties or functions. The powers exercised by those public bodies or persons may be:

- powers derived from statute;
- powers derived from the prerogative; or
- powers involving a sufficiently 'public element'.

Powers derived from statute or the prerogative

Persons or bodies that exercise powers derived from statute are generally regarded as public bodies amenable to judicial review. A major milestone was the decision in *R v Criminal Injuries Compensation Board ex p Lain* (1967), where the court confirmed that judicial review was not limited to bodies set up under statute but extended to a body exercising powers under the prerogative. However, those bodies or persons exercising powers under the prerogative are amenable to judicial review only if the issues raised are 'justiciable' (*Council of Civil Service Unions v Minister for the Civil Service* (1985) – examples of 'injusticiable' issues include foreign policy, national security and military deployments).

Powers involving a sufficiently public element

Other bodies that do not exercise powers derived from statute or the prerogative, may still be amenable to judicial review if the powers exercised are of a sufficiently public nature (*R v Panel on Take-overs and Mergers ex p Datafin Ltd* (1987)). In this milestone case, the Court of Appeal held that the Take-over Panel was amenable to judicial review despite the fact that it was a self-regulatory body operated by the City whose powers derived neither from statute nor the prerogative, and was 'without visible means of legal support'. The court indicated that in determining whether such a body was amenable to judicial review it would consider such factors as:

- the importance and public nature of its functions;
- whether its powers were underpinned by statutory provisions;
- whether it was woven into the fabric of Government regulation; and
- whether in its absence the Government would likely have had to legislate to provide for such a body.

Therefore, in *R v Advertising Standards Authority ex p The Insurance Service plc* (1990), the Advertising Standards Authority was subject to review on the basis that, in its absence, its function would have to be exercised by the Director General of Fair Trading.

As in *ex p Lain*, the court in *Datafin* stressed that in addition to looking at the *source* of the power, the court was entitled to look at the *nature* of the power.

By contrast, judicial review was not available to challenge bodies dealing with purely religious matters (*R v Chief Rabbi of the United Hebrew Congregations ex p Wachmann* (1992)), or bodies regulating horse racing (*R v Disciplinary Committee of the Jockey Club ex p Aga Khan* (1993)) or football (*R v Football Association ex p Football League* (1993)). In *ex p Wachmann*, Simon Brown J concluded that the decisions of the Chief Rabbi were not open to review because 'to attract the court's supervisory jurisdiction there must be not merely a public but potentially a governmental interest in the decision making power in question'.

Approving the decision in the *Wachmann* case, Hoffmann LJ observed in *ex p Aga Khan* that religion 'is something to be encouraged but is not the business of government'. In the latter case the Jockey Club was also found not to be subject to judicial review because it did not form part of a system of governmental control. The court was also influenced by the fact that the Club's source of power was contractual and that a private law remedy was available to the applicant. Further examples would include private educational bodies, which are unreviewable in respect of their academic policies, although state schools and colleges are reviewable.

It is a well-established principle that judicial review cannot be used to regulate the decisions of bodies that derive their authority from contract or from *a consensual submission to jurisdiction* by the parties. For example, in *R v Insurance Ombudsman Bureau ex p Aegon Life Insurance Limited* (1994), the Bureau was held not to be amenable to judicial review on the basis that its jurisdiction was dependent on the contractual consent of its members and its remedies were of a private law nature. This appears to be so even where the relevant body has monopolistic powers, or where in relation to a particular industry or activity the person concerned effectively has no choice other than to sign up to a contract to be bound by a body's rules or regulations: see *R v Panel of the Federation of Communication Services Ltd ex p Kubis* (1999), concerning dealers in the mobile telephone industry.

Judicial review of public functions only

Judicial review is only available to challenge public bodies in respect of their public functions. Judicial review therefore cannot be used to enforce a purely private law right, such as a contractual right, against a public body (*R v East Berkshire Health Authority ex p Walsh* (1985)).

Inferior courts and tribunals

Judicial review is available to challenge the lawfulness of acts or omissions by inferior courts and tribunals. The superior courts are not amenable to judicial review (that is, the High Court, the Court of Appeal and the House of Lords).

Against whom does judicial review lie?

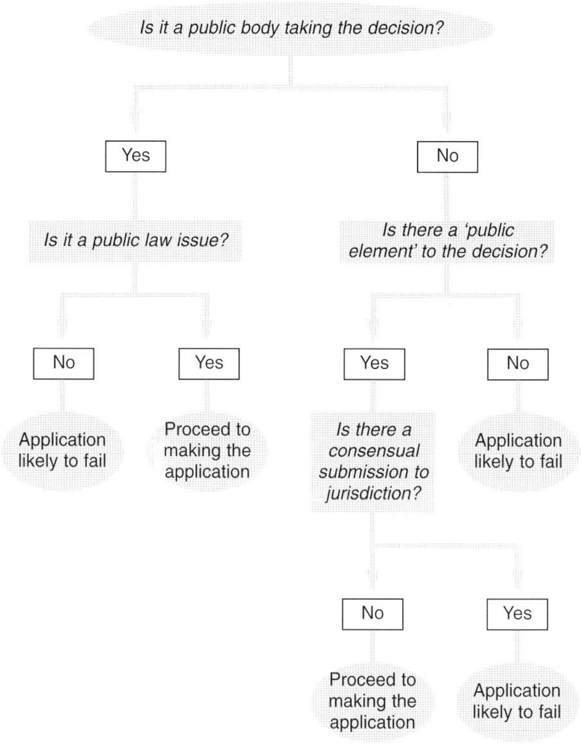

Is it a public body taking the decision?

Yes

No

Is it a public law issue?

Is there a 'public element' to the decision?

No

Application likely to fail

Yes

Proceed to making the application

Yes

Is there a consensual submission to jurisdiction?

No

Application likely to fail

No

Proceed to making the application

Yes

Application likely to fail

Is the decision, act or omission challenged amenable to judicial review?

As we have seen, r 54.1(2)(a) of the CPR provides that a claim for judicial review means a claim to review the lawfulness of:

⇒ an enactment; or
⇒ a decision, action or failure to act in relation to the exercise of a public function.

An enactment

Of course, under the doctrine of parliamentary sovereignty, the courts have no jurisdiction to question the validity of primary legislation and the courts will not investigate the internal proceedings of Parliament to investigate whether or not an Act of Parliament has been correctly enacted (*Pickin v British Railways Board* (1974)). However, the courts do have jurisdiction to determine whether an Act of Parliament is compatible with EU law, and where appropriate they must disapply conflicting provisions of domestic legislation in favour of the relevant EU provisions (*R v Secretary of State for Transport ex p Factortame (No 2)* (1990)). In addition, under the Human Rights Act (HRA) 1998, the courts have jurisdiction to determine whether an Act of Parliament is compatible with the relevant rights incorporated from the European Convention on Human Rights. However, under the HRA the courts are limited to making a declaration of incompatibility and are expressly excluded from disapplying or setting aside primary incompatible legislation.

Judicial review is available to challenge subordinate legislation on any of the grounds for review (see below). Exceptionally, the courts have declined to review subordinate legislation, despite the existence of grounds for review, in circumstances where the subordinate legislation relates to the implementation of national economic policy and is subject to the approval of Parliament: see *R v Secretary of State for the Environment ex p Hammersmith and Fulham LBC* (1991).

A decision, action or failure to act

Rule 54.1(2)(a)(ii) of the CPR provides a wide jurisdiction for the courts to control the exercise of public power. This reflects the broad view taken by the courts, in previous case law, of the measures that may be subject to judicial review. For example, the courts have granted judicial review against decisions affecting people's liberties, rights, interests, expectations, or the receipt of state benefits. The courts have also allowed claims of judicial review against other types of measures, such as 'recommendations' by doctors that mentally ill patients should be detained in hospitals (*R v Hallstrom and another ex p W* (1986)) and 'guidance' given by a Secretary of State to local authorities (*R v Secretary of State for the Environment ex p Lancashire CC* (1994)). In other cases the courts have been willing to allow claims for judicial review against policy decisions of central and local government and other public bodies, particularly where an individual's fundamental rights were affected. For example, in *R v Secretary of State for the Home Department ex p Simms* (1999), the House of Lords allowed a claim for judicial review against a blanket ban imposed by the Secretary of State on oral interviews of prisoners by journalists. Such a policy was held to be unlawful on the basis that it deprived a prisoner of a fundamental right, namely, the right to seek through oral interviews to persuade a journalist to investigate the safety of his or her conviction and to publicise any findings in an effort to gain access to justice.

In general, the courts are reluctant to impose limits upon the types of public power that are susceptible to judicial review. In circumstances where the courts consider review of the particular public power inappropriate, they are unlikely to deny the availability of judicial review but instead may indicate that it is available only in exceptional circumstances or refuse permission as a matter of discretion. In addition, even where a claim of judicial review might otherwise lie, the courts have referred to certain matters or issues as being 'injusticiable' – in that they are matters on which the courts are not equipped to judge. The most obvious example is where the exercise of a public power raises issues of national security (*Council of Civil Service Unions v Minister for the Civil Service* (1985) (the *GCHQ* case). In this case the Union was challenging the right of the Prime Minister to disallow trades unions operating at GCHQ – an organisation involved in surveillance for national security purposes. The court held that the PM's actions were reviewable but, in this case, interests of national security left the court unable to intervene. See also *R (Campaign for Nuclear Disarmament) v Prime Minister and others* (2002). Questions of foreign policy or military deployment, such as in Iraq, are examples of injusticiable matters.

Ouster clauses

A further point to note: a statute will occasionally attempt to 'oust' the jurisdiction of the court by expressly excluding decisions of certain public bodies from the scope of judicial review. The courts have construed such 'ouster clauses' strictly, and have often found ways to circumvent them. For example, in *Anisminic Ltd v Foreign Compensation Commission* (1969), s 4 of the Foreign Compensation Act 1950 excluded orders or determinations of the Foreign Compensation Commission (FCC) from judicial review. In order to circumvent the exclusion, the court held that in making a particular determination the FCC had acted outside its jurisdiction and in consequence this 'purported' determination was in fact a nullity. As a nullity, the court was able to hold that it was not entitled to the protection of the

1950 Act, which only protected 'determinations'. This interpretation was clearly contrary to Parliament's intentions.

On what grounds does judicial review lie?

- Illegality.
- Irrationality.
- Procedural impropriety.

Lord Diplock's threefold classification

In the *GCHQ* case, Lord Diplock provided a threefold classification of the grounds for judicial review:

> Judicial review has I think developed to a stage today when … one can conveniently classify under three heads the grounds on which administrative action is subject to control by judicial review. The first ground I would call '**illegality**', the second '**irrationality**' and the third '**procedural impropriety**'. That is not to say that further development on a case by case basis may not in course of time add further grounds. I have in mind particularly the possible adoption in the future of the principle of 'proportionality' which is recognised in the administrative law of several of our fellow members of the European Economic Community …

> By 'illegality' as a ground for judicial review I mean that the decision-maker must understand correctly the law that regulates his decision-making power and must give effect to it. Whether he has or not is par excellence a justiciable question to be decided, in the event of dispute, by those persons, the judges, by whom the judicial power of the state is exercisable.

> By 'irrationality' I mean what can by now be succinctly referred to as '*Wednesbury* unreasonableness' … It applies to a decision which is so outrageous in its defiance of logic or of accepted moral standards that no sensible person who had applied his mind to the question to be decided

could have arrived at it. Whether a decision falls within this category is a question that judges by their training and experience should be well equipped to answer, or else there would be something badly wrong with our judicial system. ...

I have described the third head as 'procedural impropriety' rather than failure to observe basic rules of natural justice or failure to act with procedural fairness towards the person who will be affected by the decision. This is because susceptibility to judicial review under this head covers also failure by an administrative tribunal to observe procedural rules that are expressly laid down in the legislative instrument by which its jurisdiction is conferred, even where such failure does not involve any denial of natural justice.

Lord Diplock's classification has been cited with approval in many subsequent cases. However, we should note his prediction of the development of other grounds for review. As he correctly foresaw, the principle of proportionality has increasingly been adopted as a doctrine by the domestic courts (we will examine the doctrine in connection with 'irrationality' below). Furthermore, the HRA 1998 is now generally accepted as providing a fourth ground of review, 'breach of a Convention right', though it may be argued that this ground is simply a new aspect of 'illegality'.

Illegality (doctrine of ultra vires)

Lord Diplock used the term 'illegality' to embrace a number of different grounds upon which a public body would be subject to judicial review. The most important would include:

- exceeding jurisdiction;
- failing to direct itself correctly in law (errors of law);
- failing to fulfil a statutory duty;
- acting for an improper purpose;

- failing to take into account all relevant considerations, or failing to disregard irrelevant considerations;
- delegating the exercise of discretionary powers to another unless there is clear authority to do so;
- fettering discretion;
- excessively interfering with fundamental rights.

Errors of law Regarding errors of law, previously the position was complicated by the courts differentiating between errors of law by an inferior court, or tribunal or public authority 'within jurisdiction' (which were not reviewable) and errors of law that took them outside their jurisdiction (which were reviewable). However, the general approach subsequent to the case of *Anisminic Ltd v Foreign Compensation Commission* (1969) is that almost all errors of law are now subject to judicial review. The case also made obsolete the historic distinction between errors of law on the face of the record (for example, an error in the actual order of a judge) and other errors of law (for example, an error in the reasoning behind the order). The position now is that any misdirection in law would render the relevant decision *ultra vires* and a nullity: see *Page v Hull University Visitor* (1993). However, the courts are still required to distinguish between errors of law and errors of fact. In exercising their functions, public bodies evaluate evidence and reach conclusions of fact. The court will not ordinarily interfere with the evaluation of evidence or conclusions of fact reached by a public body that has properly directed itself in law. Errors of fact will be reviewable only where the error is so excessive as to render the decision unreasonable, or the error relates to a 'jurisdictional' fact. The latter arises where the jurisdiction of the decision-maker depends on the existence of a particular fact or facts. Such facts may be described as jurisdictional or precedent facts.

Improper purpose The exercise of a discretionary power for a purpose other than that for which it was granted is unlawful. *Wheeler v Leicester City Council* (1985) provides an example of where the court found the public authority to have acted for an improper purpose. Leicester rugby club had a licence to use a recreation ground administered by the council. In 1984, three members of the club were invited to join an international rugby tour of South Africa. The council, which was vehemently opposed to sporting links with South Africa, required the club to adopt and endorse the council's anti-apartheid stance and actively to campaign against the international tour and dissuade its members from participating in such a tour. The club stated that it agreed with the council in condemning apartheid in South Africa, but indicated that its role in relation to its members was purely advisory and that it was neither unlawful nor contrary to the rules of the club for members to join the tour. Subsequently, the three members took part in the tour. In response the council passed a resolution banning the club and its members from using the recreation ground for 12 months. The House of Lords held that the council's use of its statutory power to ban the club was a misuse of power because its purpose was to punish the club when it had done no wrong. See also *Congreve v Home Office* (1976).

An authority may act for mixed motives, some authorised and some not. The general approach of the courts in such situations is to hold that the action will be lawful if the authorised purpose is the true and dominant one. On the other hand, if the unlawful purpose materially influences the decision-maker, the action will be unlawful because irrelevant considerations will have been taken into account. See *R v Inner London Education Authority ex p Westminster City Council* (1986). There is often overlap between acting for an improper purpose and failing to take into account relevant considerations, or failing to disregard irrelevant considerations.

Relevant and irrelevant considerations A public authority's powers must be exercised consistent with the conferring statute. The exercise of a power will be unlawful where, on a proper construction of the relevant statute, the decision-maker has failed to take account of relevant considerations, or has taken into account irrelevant considerations. What is or is not a relevant consideration in any case will vary greatly according to the context.

The courts have held that local authorities can take into account their own limited resources in deciding whether they owe a duty to make provisions for the needs of an individual (*R v Gloucestershire County Council ex p Barry* (1997)). However, the impact on an individual's fundamental rights is also a relevant consideration.

An order of a magistrate or tribunal taking irrelevant factors into account, or failing to have regard to relevant factors, will be quashed (*R v Horseferry Road Magistrates' Court ex p Pearson* (1976)). Similarly, the immigration authorities must have regard to relevant factors and ignore irrelevant factors in the exercise of their statutory powers (*R v Immigration Appeal Tribunal ex p Bastiampillai* (1983)).

Unlawful delegation and fettering discretion Decision-makers may also have acted unlawfully if they fail to retain their decision-making power. Decision-makers may fail to retain discretion in one of two ways. First, they might delegate their decision-making power to someone else, contrary to the maxim *delegatus non potest delegare*. The rule is that a statutory power must be exercised only by the body or officer on whom it has been conferred, unless delegation is expressly authorised by the statutory words or by necessary implication.

However, in *Carltona Ltd v Commissioner of Works* (1943), the court held it to be acceptable for a senior official to sign the actual notice requisitioning a factory in time of war, even though the power of requisition had been given to a body headed by a minister, on the basis that the minister was accountable for the actions of the civil servant under the convention of ministerial responsibility. Similarly, in *Oladehinde v Secretary of State for the Home Department* (1990), the House of Lords held that the Secretary of State could validly authorise immigration inspectors to take decisions on his behalf to deport persons from the United Kingdom under the Immigration Act 1971. Generally, the powers of public authorities are lawfully exercisable by their servants or agents. Furthermore, local authority functions may be delegated either to officers, or to committees or sub-committees of the authority. Courts will have regard to considerations of practical convenience.

Secondly, decision-makers must not 'fetter' their discretion by adopting an over-rigid rule or policy in relation to its exercise. An authority may legitimately adopt general rules or policies in relation to the exercise of its discretion, provided they are consistent with the purpose of the enabling legislation and not unjust. However, the authority must be prepared to consider making an exception to the general rule if the circumstances of a particular case warrant it. In *British Oxygen Co Ltd v Minister of Technology* (1971), BOC applied for a grant under statutory provisions to fund the purchase of metal cylinders required to store pressurised gases, which it manufactured. Individually the cylinders cost £20. The Board of Trade had a policy of denying grants for plant items costing less than £25 and decided that the cylinders were not eligible for a grant. In giving judgment Lord Reid stated:

> The general rule is that anyone who has to exercise a statutory discretion must not 'shut [his] ears to the application' (to quote from Bankes LJ in *R v Port of London*

Authority ex p Kynoch Ltd (1919)). I do not think that there is any great difference between a policy and a rule. There may be cases where an officer or authority ought to listen to a substantial argument reasonably presented urging a change of policy. What the authority must not do is to refuse to listen at all. But a Ministry or large authority may have had to deal already with a multitude of similar applications and then they will almost certainly have evolved a policy so precise that it could well be called a rule. There can be no objection to that provided the authority is always willing to listen to anyone with something new to say …

In *British Oxygen* the court held that the Board of Trade had adequately considered the merits of BOC's application and therefore had not applied its policy in an over-rigid manner.

Illegality under the Human Rights Act 1998 As has already been mentioned, following the implementation of the HRA 1998, a new category of challenge has been introduced that could be put under the general banner of 'illegality', or alternatively regarded as a free-standing ground for challenge.

The only exceptions to the obligations imposed on public authorities by the HRA 1998 to comply with Convention rights are set out in s 6(2), that is, where:

- the authority could not have acted differently; or
- the authority was acting under primary legislation and that legislation cannot be given effect in a way that is compatible with Convention rights.

In deciding whether a decision or action is compatible with a Convention right, a judge will need to consider several factors:

- whether a Convention right is raised and whether it has been interfered with;

➲ whether that interference is 'in accordance with the law' or 'prescribed by law';

➲ whether the interference serves a legitimate aim as listed in some of the Convention Articles. For example, Article 10 defines legitimate aims as:

> … formalities, conditions, restrictions or penalties as are prescribed by law and are necessary in a democratic society, in the interests of national security, territorial integrity or public safety, for the prevention of disorder or crime, for the protection of health or morals, for the protection of the reputation or rights of others, for preventing the disclosure of information received in confidence, or for maintaining the authority and impartiality of the judiciary.

Finally, the judge will need to assess whether the interference is proportionate to the aim pursued. See the comments on proportionality below.

Irrationality

Irrationality and the Wednesbury principle Prior to Lord Diplock's third classification of 'irrationality' (see above), this ground for review was traditionally referred to as '*Wednesbury* unreasonableness'. A decision of a public authority is open to challenge on this ground if the court is satisfied that the decision is 'so unreasonable that no authority could ever come to it' or 'so absurd that no sensible person could ever dream that it lay within the powers of the authority' (*Associated Provincial Picture Houses Ltd v Wednesbury Corporation* (1948)). In effect, the ground provides a limited basis for the courts to challenge a decision on its 'merits'. However, the level of review inherent in the *Wednesbury* principle is notoriously low. The threshold of 'irrationality' is a high one, and in the past the courts have been very reluctant to hold that a decision-maker crossed it.

Nevertheless, in recent years the courts have shown themselves to be more willing to question the rationality of decisions, particularly in circumstances where an individual's fundamental rights are in play. No doubt this was partly in anticipation of the incorporation of Convention rights under the HRA 1998. The courts developed a principle of 'anxious scrutiny' or 'super-*Wednesbury*' review where such rights were in play. The principle is that where fundamental rights are adversely affected, the court will require more by way of justification before it is satisfied that a decision was reasonable. In *R v Ministry of Defence ex p Smith* (1996), the court reviewed a decision to discharge a number of individuals from the army on the basis of their homosexuality. The Government's core argument was that the presence of homosexuals in the armed forces would have a substantial and negative effect on the operational effectiveness of the armed forces. With some reluctance, the Court of Appeal held that the decision of the Ministry of Defence was justifiable, but approved the following approach:

> The court may not interfere with the exercise of an administrative discretion on substantive grounds save where the court is satisfied that the decision is unreasonable in the sense that it is beyond the range of responses open to a reasonable decision-maker. But in judging whether the decision-maker has exceeded this margin of appreciation the human rights context is important. The more substantial the interference with human rights, the more the court will require by way of justification before it is satisfied that the decision is reasonable in the sense outlined above.

It should be noted that subsequently the applicants took their case to Strasbourg and, in *Smith v United Kingdom (No 1)* (1999), the ECtHR held that there had been a violation of Article 8 ECHR (right to private life) and Article 13 ECHR (right to an effective remedy). The Court held that the 'irrationality' test in judicial review provided an insufficiently effective means of scrutiny in the circumstances. This questioning by the ECtHR of judicial review as an 'effective remedy' in this and a number of other cases has been the source of much debate.

Proportionality Since the HRA 1998 came into force, there has been considerable discussion about its impact upon the *Wednesbury* test. The law in this area is still developing, but the position appears to be that where a breach of a Convention right is in issue, the traditional test is no longer applicable and its place taken by a new test of *proportionality* adopted from European jurisprudence.

Proportionality is not entirely alien to judges in the UK. In *R v Goldstein* (1983), Lord Diplock famously summarised the concept into everyday language: 'You must not use a steam hammer to crack a nut, if a nutcracker would do.' However, the test for proportionality adopted from EC law and from the jurisprudence of the ECtHR is considerably more developed and complex. The courts will ask:

- whether the action pursued a legitimate aim;
- whether the means adopted to achieve that aim were appropriate;
- whether less restrictive means could have been adopted to achieve that aim; and
- whether overall the interference with an individual's rights is justified in the interests of a democratic society.

The House of Lords considered the impact of the HRA 1998 on judicial review in *R (Daly) v Secretary of State for the Home Department* (2001), and in particular the difference between *Wednesbury* unreasonableness and proportionality. Lord Steyn observed that the intensity of review was greater under the proportionality approach. Whilst in many cases there is an overlap between the traditional grounds of review and the approach of proportionality, he suggested that there were three concrete differences:

> First, the doctrine of proportionality may require the reviewing court to assess the balance which the decision maker had struck, not merely whether it is within the range of rational or reasonable decisions. Secondly, the proportionality test may go further than the traditional grounds of review inasmuch as it may require attention to be directed to the relative weight accorded to interests and considerations. Thirdly, even the heightened scrutiny test developed in *Smith* is not necessarily appropriate to the protection of human rights.

In addition, Lord Cooke commented,

> I think the day will come when it will be more widely recognised that [the *Wednesbury* case] was an unfortunately retrogressive decision in English administrative law, in so far as it suggested that there are degrees of reasonableness and that only a very extreme degree can bring an administrative decision within the legitimate scope of judicial invalidation

However, in *British Civilian Internees Far Eastern Region v Secretary of State for Defence* (2003), the Court of Appeal held that until the House of Lords expressly declared otherwise, the *Wednesbury* test does continue to survive, and is the correct test to apply in a case which does not involve Community law and does not engage any question of rights under the ECHR.

Procedural impropriety

Grounds for judicial review exist:

- where there has been a breach of the common law rules of natural justice; or

- where there has been procedural unfairness; or
- where there has been a failure to comply with any statutory procedural obligations; and
- where an applicant has a legitimate expectation of being treated in a certain way by a public authority, even though there is no other legal basis to support a claim for such treatment.

Natural justice

Natural justice comprises three basic principles:

- No man is to be a judge in his own cause (*nemo judex in causa sua*).
- No man is to be condemned unheard (*audi alteram partem*).
- A decision-maker has a general duty to act fairly.

These rules are concerned with the manner in which the decision is taken rather than with whether or not the decision is correct.

Natural justice and procedural fairness   Historically, the common law rules of natural justice developed in relation to decision-making in the courts. Therefore, traditionally the principles were applied only in proceedings concerning judicial or quasi-judicial decisions. However, in *Ridge v Baldwin* (1964) the obligation to observe natural justice was held to extend to administrative decision-making. In *Ridge*, the court held that a police authority's decision to dismiss a chief constable was procedurally unfair in that it failed to provide the applicant with a proper opportunity to challenge allegations made against him.

In determining the standards required of a decision-making process, the judges have used the terms 'natural justice' and 'fairness' interchangeably. They favour the use of the latter, particularly when denoting the standards required in administrative decision-taking. See *Re K (H) (An Infant)* (1967).

It must be remembered that the rules of natural justice, or of fairness, are not 'cut and dried'. They vary infinitely, as Lord Denning put it in *R v Secretary of State for the Home Department ex p Santillo* (1981). What fairness demands will depend upon the nature of the individual's interest, the impact of the decision, whether the decision is preliminary or final, the subject matter of the decision, the terms of any relevant statutory provisions and all the circumstances of the case. For example, decisions over the granting of licences will depend upon the status of the applicant. In *McInnes v Onslow Fane* (1978), the court indicated that procedural protections are at their highest where the decision deals with the forfeiture of a licence and at their lowest where the decision deals with a mere first-time application for a licence. A higher standard will normally apply where the relevant decision affects a person's fundamental rights, or liberty or property, or where a person is dismissed from public office.

In general, it may be said that the required standards of fairness will rise as one moves from merely administrative decisions towards decisions exercising a judicial or quasi-judicial function. See *Doody v Secretary of State for the Home Department* (1993), where the courts considered the standards of fairness to which mandatory life prisoners were entitled in respect of the decision made by the Secretary of State when fixing the penal element in a mandatory life sentence.

Examples of procedural requirements Procedural protections might include the right to be given prior notice of a decision. See *Cooper v Wandsworth Board of Works* (1863), where Cooper was entitled to be given prior notice of an intention to knock down his house. The court may require that sufficient time be given to prepare a case in response to allegations. In *R v Thames Magistrates Court ex p Polemis* (1974), the decision by a magistrate to refuse an adjournment, requested by Polemis to respond to a criminal charge for which he had received the summons only that morning, was quashed. The maxim *audi alteram partem* requires that every person be given a fair hearing; whether that includes an oral hearing depends upon the possible sanctions to be imposed upon the applicant and the likelihood that oral evidence would help to resolve issues of fact: see *R v Army Board of Defence Council ex p Anderson* (1991). In *R v Secretary of State for the Home Department ex p Tarrant* (1984), the court indicated that the applicant might have a right to request legal representation depending on such issues as the seriousness of the charge and whether points of law are raised, but also the need for reasonable speed in the adjudication. There might also arise a duty for the decision-maker to give reasons, to show that the matter has been properly considered, but the courts will not impose such a duty where it might place an undue burden on the decision-maker.

Some statutes prescribe procedural requirements for the exercise of a particular statutory power. For example, there may be provisions for the composition of a decision-making board, or obligations to consult, or to conduct an inquiry, or to consider objections, or to give reasons for a decision. Where a statute provides a mandatory procedure it must be followed. However, it appears that where a provision is construed as merely *directory*, substantial compliance will suffice (*Coney v Choyce* (1975)).

Note that Article 6 ECHR provides particular rights where a pubic authority makes a 'determination of civil rights and obligations'. An applicant is entitled to:

- a fair and public hearing within a reasonable time;
- an independent and impartial tribunal established by law;
- judgment pronounced publicly, unless the public interest overrides such a right.

Legitimate expectation A person may have a legitimate expectation that that he or she will be given a hearing, or consulted before a decision is taken. Such a legitimate expectation might arise because an applicant has relied on a promise or previous conduct by a public authority. In the *GCHQ* case, the court indicated that the Unions had a legitimate expectation of being consulted prior to the implementation of major changes affecting the staff, but in the particular circumstances, the interests of national security overrode those legitimates expectations. In exceptional circumstances, a legitimate expectation may not merely ensure that the individual is consulted but may even ensure that a benefit he or she enjoys is not removed. In *R v North and East Devon Health Authority ex p Coughlan* (2000), a disabled applicant had been given a clear promise that a nursing home would be her 'home for life'. Subsequently the home was closed by the local authority. The court held that the decision of the authority was unfair on the basis that it frustrated the applicant's legitimate expectation. It may be argued that the doctrine of legitimate expectation is being expanded here not only to supervise the manner by which a decision is reached, but also to require the authority to reach a particular decision. This aspect of the doctrine is likely to develop on a case-by-case basis.

The rule against bias *Nemo judex in sua causa* ('No one should be a judge in his own cause') is taken to mean that adjudicators must not have (or be seen to have) a pecuniary, family or professional interest in the outcome of a decision.

There are two broad categories of case:

⇨ where the adjudicator has either a direct pecuniary or a proprietary interest in the matter; and

⇨ where there is a non-pecuniary interest, such as a friendship or professional connection, or there is an appearance of bias by reason of conduct or behaviour.

In the first category of case there is an irrebuttable presumption of bias and the adjudicator is automatically disqualified (*Dimes v Grand Junction Canal Proprietors* (1852)). This category of case was recently extended in *R v Bow Street Metropolitan Stipendiary Magistrate ex p Pinochet Ugarte (No 2)* (1999). The House of Lords held that automatic disqualification was not limited to cases where there was a pecuniary or proprietary interest, but would also apply in cases where the judge's decision would lead to the promotion of a cause in which the judge was involved together with one of the parties. The Law Lords had ruled (by a majority of 3:2) that Pinochet did not enjoy immunity from arrest pursuant to international warrants to enable extradition to Spain. Amnesty International had been allowed to intervene in the proceedings; they clearly supported the cause for extradition. Lord Hoffman (one of the Law Lords hearing the case) chaired a charity (AIC), a sub-organisation within Amnesty International. On the basis of this involvement, the House of Lords ruled that he was automatically disqualified and set aside their earlier decision.

In the second category, the adjudicator will be disqualified where there is a 'real danger' of bias on his or her part (*R v Gough* (1993)). It is generally unnecessary to establish the presence of actual bias. A modest adjustment to the 'real danger' test was adopted by the House of Lords in *Porter v Magill* (2002). The adjustment reflected concerns that the test as it stood put too great an emphasis on the court's view of the danger of bias rather than the view of an ordinary observer. Lord Phillips' formulation in *Re Medicaments and Related Classes of Goods (No 2)* (2001) was cited with approval:

> The court must first ascertain all the circumstances which have a bearing on the suggestion that the judge was biased. It must then ask whether those circumstances would lead a fair-minded and informed observer to conclude that there was a real possibility, or a real danger, the two being the same, that the tribunal was biased.

Standing: who can apply for judicial review?

Procedural bars: exclusivity principle An application for judicial review must surmount special procedural bars designed to protect public authorities. In particular, the applicant must satisfy the requirements of permission, standing and a short time limit. These protections are said to be necessary in order to prevent disruption to administrative processes without good cause and to ensure that the Administrative Court is not overburdened with inappropriate claims.

Consequently, in *O'Reilly v Mackman* (1983) it was held that it was contrary to public policy and an abuse of process for an individual to use a private action to challenge a decision by a public body on the basis that it infringed rights protected in public law, since to do so would avoid the procedural restraints imposed on an application for judicial review.

However this 'exclusivity principle' has been criticised in so far as it has led to the striking out of meritorious cases on purely procedural grounds. As a consequence, more recent case law has avoided its rigid application, particularly where cases involve both public and private law elements (*Roy v Kensington and Chelsea and Westminster Family Practitioner Committee* (1992)). Furthermore, in *Trustees of the Dennis*

Rye Pension Fund v Sheffield City Council (1997), Lord Woolf MR, while confirming the general rule that the procedural constraints should not be avoided, nonetheless indicated that the court should not be overly concerned with the distinction between public and private law rights, and that a court should be slow to strike out a case on the basis of the exclusivity principle, particularly if the choice of proceedings had 'no significant disadvantages' for the parties. For example, if a claim were brought by way of private proceedings when it should have been brought by way of judicial review, but the applicant would nonetheless have satisfied the requirements of permission in an application for judicial review, that would be an indication that there was no significant disadvantage to the public authority. See also *Clark v University of Lincolnshire and Humberside* (2000).

The test for permission   Section 31(3) of the Supreme Court Act 1981 provides that the court will not grant permission to proceed with a claim for judicial review 'unless it considers that the applicant has a sufficient interest in the matter to which the application relates'.

The test for sufficient interest or standing involves a two-stage process:

⮕ The courts will consider an application for permission in the first instance without a hearing and on the basis of the papers before them. The purpose at this stage is to eliminate hopeless, frivolous or vexatious cases and to ensure that it is a claim fit for further consideration at a substantive hearing. The courts generally avoid making a detailed assessment of standing at this stage, except to filter out claimants who are no more than 'meddlesome busybodies' (*R v Monopolies and Mergers Commission ex p Argyll Group plc* (1986)).

⮕ If permission is granted at that stage, the court may revisit the question of standing at the substantive hearing where it may be considered in the light of the full factual and legal context of the claim (*R* v *Inland Revenue Commissioners ex p National Federation of Self-employed and Small Businesses Ltd* (1982)).

Standing In considering the question of 'sufficient interest', the court considers the relationship of the claimant to the matter and all the circumstances of the case. If the claimant has a direct personal interest in the matter then generally he or she will have sufficient interest. The courts have taken a broad approach to what constitutes a 'personal' interest. Individuals affected by the action or decision in question will normally have standing. For example, in *R* v *Her Majesty's Treasury ex p Smedley* (1985), a taxpayer had sufficient standing to challenge a government undertaking to pay a contribution to the European Community. In *R* v *Selby District Council ex p Samuel Smith Old Breweries* (2000), a landowner within a greenbelt in the vicinity of a proposed development had sufficient standing, even though not directly affected by the development.

Even where there is no direct or personal interest, the court may still exercise its discretion to grant permission where a public-spirited claimant seeks to raise a matter of general or public interest. For example, in *R* v *Secretary of State for Foreign and Commonwealth Affairs ex p Rees-Mogg* (1993), Lord Rees-Mogg was granted permission to challenge the lawfulness of the UK's ratification of the Treaty on European Union, though the claim failed at the substantive stage.

Claims for judicial review are often made by representative bodies campaigning on particular issues. The courts have taken an increasingly liberal approach to standing in these types of application. In *R v Secretary of State for Social Services ex p Child Poverty Action Group* (1990), the CPAG was held to have standing sufficient to commence proceedings relating to the interpretation of social security legislation. Where there is a strong public interest case, pressure groups have been granted standing. Greenpeace had sufficient interest to seek review of an inspectorate's decisions relating to radioactive waste from Sellafield. On the question of whether or not to grant standing, judges appear influenced by factors such as the likely absence of any other challenger, the expertise of the challenger, the importance of vindicating the rule of law and the prominence of the challenger as an adviser on the relevant matters. In *R v Secretary of State for Foreign and Commonwealth Affairs ex p World Development Movement* (1995), the WDM had sufficient standing to seek review of the Foreign Secretary's decision to use overseas aid money to fund the Pergau Dam project in Malaysia. The applicants were advisers on overseas aid, and in their absence there was no other challenger with the expertise to question the viability of the project. By contrast, in *R v Secretary of State for the Environment ex p Rose Theatre Trust Co* (1990), the pressure group was refused standing despite its being set up to preserve the remains of the Rose Theatre. It was argued there was no legal merit to the group's case. The decision was criticised by Sedley J in *R v Somerset County Council ex p Dixon* (1997), where he stated:

> Public law is not at base about rights, even though abuses of power may and often do invade private rights; it is about wrongs – that is to say misuses of public power; and the courts have always been alive to the fact that a person or organisation with no particular stake in the issue or the outcome may, without in any sense being a mere meddler, wish and be well placed to call the attention of the court to an apparent misuse of public power.

Human Rights Act: 'sufficient interest' and 'victim' tests

Where judicial review is on grounds of breach of a Convention right, the current 'sufficient interest' test will have to be reconciled with the test under the HRA 1998. Section 7 of the Act requires that only a 'victim' (as per Article 34 ECHR) may rely on Convention rights. This would appear to exclude challenges by representative bodies or pressure groups on human rights.

To assess the position requires reference to the relevant case law of the ECtHR. 'Victim' appears to cover both those directly affected and those 'at risk' of being affected. In *Campbell and Cosans v UK* (1982), children attending a school where corporal punishment was practised were treated as 'victims' even though they had not been punished. In *Sutherland v UK* (1998), an applicant claimed that the age of consent for homosexuals in the UK violated his rights under Article 8 ECHR. He had never been prosecuted, nor had the domestic authorities expressed any interest in doing so, nonetheless it was held that he was directly affected and therefore could claim to be a victim for the purposes of the Convention. It appears, however, that there must be a reasonable likelihood that the applicant would be subject to the impugned measure.

In addition, representative bodies have qualified as victims in certain cases. Unincorporated associations may be regarded as 'victims'. In *Christians Against Racism and Fascism v UK* (1980), a broad association of religious groups was regarded as a 'victim' when a procession it planned was banned. However, representative bodies campaigning on behalf of others are unlikely to satisfy the victim test.

It is possible that a challenge by way of judicial review may involve both Convention and standard grounds. In such cases it may be that the applicant will face two separate tests.

Delay A procedural bar of great practical significance is the requirement that a claim for judicial review must be made promptly, and in any event within three months from the date upon which the claim arose (CPR r 54.5). This may be contrasted with the six-year limitation that applies to ordinary civil litigation.

The test is promptness, and this may not be satisfied simply because the claim is brought within the three-month time limit (*R v Independent Television Commission ex p TV NI Ltd* (1991)). The 'promptness' test may yet be open to challenge on the grounds that it breaches requirements under the ECHR: see *R v Hammersmith and Fulham LBC ex p Burkett* (2002).

The court retains a discretion to grant permission even where a claim is not brought within the three-month time limit. However, the courts have recognised that public law claims require strict adherence to the time limits relating to judicial review proceedings (*R v Institute of Chartered Accountants in England and Wales ex p Andreou* (1996)).

Under the old rules for judicial review (RSC Ord 53) the courts refused to extend the time limit where the delay was the fault of the claimant's lawyers (see *R v Secretary of State for Health ex p Furneaux* (1994)). However, other factors outside the claimant's control, such as delay in getting legal help, may provide a good reason for extending the time limit (*R v Stratford-upon-Avon District Council ex p Jackson* (1985)). The courts may accept that there is a good reason if the claimant was unaware of the decision or action under challenge, provided he or she applied expeditiously once he or she was aware of it (see *R v Secretary of State for Transport ex p Presvac Engineering Ltd* (1991) and *R v Secretary of State for the Home Department ex p Ruddock* (1987)). The courts will be more inclined to grant an extension where issues of general public importance are raised (for example, 'phone tapping' in *ex p Ruddock*).

Even where there are good reasons to excuse a delay, the court may still refuse permission, or refuse to grant a remedy at the substantive hearing, if it considers it inappropriate to do so on the basis of prejudice to third parties or detriment to good administration (see *R v Dairy Produce Quota Tribunal ex p Caswell* (1990) and *R v Brent LBC ex p O'Malley* (1997)).

Other reasons for refusing permission The granting of permission is a matter of discretion, and the court will not normally grant permission where the claimant has an adequate alternative remedy available. For example, where a structure for appeal exists under statute, judicial review should not be used as a means of circumventing this (see *R v Secretary of State for Social Services ex p Connolly* (1986)). Exceptionally the court may grant permission, even where an alternative remedy is available, if there is some other reason why judicial review proceedings are appropriate: see, for example, *R v Hereford Magistrates' Court ex p Rowlands* (1998). Permission may also be refused where the claim is purely academic, or where the claimant has suffered no real injustice.

Remedies

In a claim for judicial review the court may grant one of the following remedies:

- The *prerogative* orders (CPR r 54.2):
    - quashing order (formerly *certiorari*);
    - prohibiting order (formerly *order of prohibition*);
    - mandatory order (formerly *mandamus*).

⮑ Other remedies (CPR r 54.3):
- injunctions;
- declarations;
- damages.

Prerogative orders

⮑ A *quashing order* quashes an unlawful decision of a public authority. Where a decision is quashed the court has power to remit the matter back to the decision-maker.

⮑ A *prohibiting order* restrains a public authority from acting outside its jurisdiction or otherwise abusing its powers.

⮑ A *mandatory order* requires a public authority to carry out its judicial or other public duty. A mandatory order cannot be used against the Crown (s 40 of the Crown Proceedings Act 1947) but can be used against a minister of the Crown (see *M v Home Office* (1994)).

Other remedies

⮑ Section 31(2) of the SCA 1981 provides that, in a claim for judicial review, the courts may grant an *injunction* (including interim injunctions) or a *declaration*, either in addition to or instead of the prerogative orders, where it is 'just and convenient' to do so. A declaration is a statement of the legal position in the matter before the court. It may simply declare the true construction of a statute, or that an administrative act is invalid. A declaration lacks coercive power, but public authorities will normally respond to a declaration by rectifying their actions.

⮑ *Damages* may be awarded in conjunction with any of the other remedies, but a claimant may not seek damages alone in a claim for judicial review. Furthermore, damages will be awarded only if they could have been awarded in an ordinary claim, that is, in a private law claim or a claim under the HRA 1998. See, for example, *R v Enfield Borough Council ex p Bernard* (2002). In other words, the judicial review procedure does not create any new right to damages, but simply provides a means to claim damages which otherwise would have to be claimed in separate proceedings.